Bertolt Brecht
POETRY AND PROSE

The German Library: Volume 75

Volkmar Sander, General Editor

EDITORIAL BOARD
Peter Demetz (Yale University)
Reinhold Grimm (University of California)
Jost Hermand (University of Wisconsin)
Patricia A. Herminghouse (University of Rochester)
Walter Hinderer (Princeton University)
Victor Lange (Princeton University)†
Frank G. Ryder (University of Virginia)†
Wolfgang Schirmacher (The New School for Social Research)
A. Leslie Willson (University of Texas)

Bertolt Brecht
POETRY AND PROSE

Edited by Reinhold Grimm
with the Collaboration of
Caroline Molina y Vedia

CONTINUUM
NEW YORK · LONDON

2003
The Continuum International Publishing Group Inc
15 East 26 Street, New York, NY 10010

The Continuum International Publishing Group Ltd
The Tower Building, 11 York Road, London SE1 7NX

The German Library is published
in cooperation with Deutsches Haus, New York University.
This volume has been supported by Inter Nationes.

Copyright © 2003 by The Continuum International Publishing Group Inc
Introduction © 2003 by Reinhold Grimm

All rights reserved. No part of this book may be reproduced,
stored in a retrieval system, or transmitted, in any form or
by any means, electronic, mechanical, photocopying, recording,
or otherwise, without the written permission of the publishers.

Printed in the United States of America

Library of Congress Cataloging-in-Publication Data

Brecht, Bertolt, 1898–1956.
  [Selections. English & German. 2003]
  Bertolt Brecht : poetry and prose / edited by Reinhold Grimm with the collaboration of Caroline Molina y Vedia.
      p. cm. — (German library ; v. 75)
  German and English on facing pages.
  ISBN 0-8264-1504-0 (hardcover : alk. paper) — ISBN 0-8264-1505-9 (pbk. : alk. paper)
     1. Grimm, Reinhold.   II. Molina y Vedia, Caroline.   III. Title.
  IV. Series.
  PT2603.R397A2   2003
  832'.912—dc22

                                                            2003014549

Acknowledgments will be found on page 149,
which constitutes an extension of the copyright page.

Contents

Bertolt Brecht—A Modern Classic? by Reinhold Grimm   xiii

PART 1
POETRY

Prelude

O Lust des Beginnens / On the Joy of Beginning   4
Translated by Humphrey Milnes

From *Bertolt Brecht's Domestic Breviary* (1927)

Von der Freundlichkeit der Welt / Of the Friendliness of the World   8
Translated by Karl Neumann

Großer Dankchoral / Great Hymn of Thanksgiving   8
Translated by Karl Neumann

Erinnerung an die Marie A. / Remembering Marie A.   10
Translated by John Willett

Ballade von der Hanna Cash / Ballad of Hanna Cash   12
Translated by John Willett

Von der Kindesmörderin Marie Farrar / On the Infanticide Marie Farrar   18
Translated by Sidney H. Bremer

Gesang des Soldaten der roten Armee /
Song of the Soldier of the Red Army   24
Translated by John Willett

Von des Cortez Leuten / Of Cortez's Men   28
Translated by Frank Jellinek

Vom armen B.B. / Of Poor B.B.   30
Translated by Michael Hamburger

From Poems Written between 1913 and 1926

Der Nachgeborene / Born Later   38
Translated by Michael Hamburger

Der 4. Psalm / The Fourth Psalm   38
Translated by Christopher Middleton

Entdeckung an einer jungen Frau /
Discovery about a Young Woman   40
Translated by John Willett

From **Poems Written between 1926 and 1933**

Vier Aufforderungen an einen Mann von verschiedener Seite zu verschiedenen Zeiten / Four Invitations to a Man at Different Times from Different Quarters   44
Translated by Frank Jellinek

Das Frühjahr / The Spring   46
Translated by John Willett

Die Nachtlager / A Bed for the Night   46
Translated by George Rapp

Von allen Werken / Of All the Works of Man   48
Team Translation

Contents • vii

From *Poems* Written between 1933 and 1938

Ausschließlich wegen der zunehmenden Unordnung /
Solely because of the Increasing Disorder 54
Translated by Frank Jellinek

Über die Gewalt / On Violence 54
Translated by John Willett

From *Svendborg Poems* (1939)

Auf der Mauer stand mit Kreide / On the Wall Was Chalked 58
Team Translation

General, dein Tank ist ein starker Wagen /
General, Your Tank Is a Powerful Vehicle 58
Translated by Lee Baxandall

Lied der Starenschwärme / Song of the Flocks of Starlings 58
Translated by Michael Hamburger

Der Pflaumenbaum / The Plum Tree 60
Team Translation

Fragen eines lesenden Arbeiters /
Questions from a Worker Who Reads 62
Translated by Michael Hamburger

Legende von der Entstehung des Buches Taoteking auf dem Weg des Laotse in die Emigration / Legend of the Origin of the Book Tao-Te-Ching on Lao-Tsu's Road into Exile 64
Translated by John Willett

An die Nachgeborenen / To Those Born Later 70
Team Translation

Interlude
Poems (Songs) from and about Plays

Das Lied von der Moldau / The Song of the Moldau 80
Translated by Max Knight and Joseph Fabry

Lied vom achten Elefanten / Song of the Eighth Elephant   80
Translated by Ralph Manheim

Das Lied vom Sankt Nimmerleinstag / The Song of Saint Neverkin's Day   82
Translated by Ralph Manheim

Lied des Stückschreibers / The Playwright's Song   84
Translated by John Willett

From *Poems* Written between 1938 and 1941

Schlechte Zeit für Lyrik / Bad Time for Poetry   94
Team Translation

Sonett Nr. 1 / Sonnet No. 1   94
Translated by John Willett

1940 VI / 1940 VI   96
Translated by Sammy McLean

From *Poems* Written between 1941 and 1947

Die Landschaft des Exils / Landscape of Exile   100
Translated by H. R. Hays

Nachdenkend über die Hölle / On Thinking about Hell   100
Translated by Nicholas Jacobs

Der demokratische Richter / The Democratic Judge   102
Translated by Michael Hamburger

Kinderkreuzzug / Children's Crusade   104
Translated by H. R. Hays

Die Maske des Bösen / The Mask of Evil   114
Translated by H. R. Hays

From *Poems* Written between 1947 and 1956

Auf einen chinesischen Theewurzellöwen /
On a Chinese Carving of a Lion   118
Team Translation

Der Radwechsel / Changing the Wheel   118
Translated by Michael Hamburger

Die Lösung / The Solution   118
Translated by Derek Bowman

Der Rauch / The Smoke   120
Translated by Derek Bowman

Postlude

Alles wandelt sich / Everything Changes   124
Translated by John Willett

PART 2
PROSE

From *Tales from the Calendar*

Socrates Wounded   129
Translated by Yvonne Kapp

The Unseemly Old Lady   144
Translated by Yvonne Kapp

Introduction

Bertolt Brecht—A Modern Classic?

Let us begin with Dante Alighieri, with whom Bertolt Brecht was not altogether unfamiliar.

The political turmoil in Florence in the thirteenth and early fourteenth centuries—that is, the dispute between the Guelfs and the Ghibellines in which Dante was so deeply embroiled, and which drove him into exile for decades—all this is just a piece of local history that lies far in the past. Dante's *Divine Comedy,* however, has remained one of the greatest testaments of world literature for over half a millennium.

To get an idea of Brecht and his importance in light of the most recent geopolitical events—specifically, the fall of a kind of socialism that never "actually existed," but that took decades of laborious effort to construct—it will suffice to recall a Brechtian anecdote which, in its day, seemed almost disconcerting. When asked what would ever become of his writing, which was so obviously meant for a capitalistic society and could only be seen as antiquated and useless in a socialistic one, the dialectician (who had long since referred to himself as a "[modern] classic") replied coolly: "My texts and theories are valid for a bourgeois, a capitalist society; they are also valid for socialist, communist, classless societies—and for all other forms of society in the future." To be sure, the historical "turning point" *(Wende)* of 1989 came about quite differently than Brecht had expected or wished. But for his writing and its towering status within world literature, that historical event and its repercussions have just as much or as little importance as Dante's political engagement and subsequently destroyed hopes.

Only in such a double perspective—as a temporally bound historical phenomenon and as a larger, lasting literary testament of classical dimensions—can the life and work of Bertolt Brecht be wholly understood and justly evaluated.

* * *

There can be no doubt that Brecht's basic experience of life was one of chaos. He experienced the universe as a seething hubbub of disorder: a desolate yet pleasurable frenzy out of which the individual emerges and into which he disappears again without a trace. Vultures and sharks, greased hangman's nooses and rotting wrecks, drunkards, pirates, and soldiers make up this world. Highly compelling is the image of the primeval forest, the all-nourishing, all-devouring jungle. This mythical forest is everywhere. In *In the Jungle of Cities* (one of Brecht's early plays), the same blind chaos rages that rages under the dripping leafy treetops of the jungle. The asphalt jungle and the tropical thicket intertwine.

The insatiable desire with which Brecht absorbed this experience of the world has often been documented. Even during his exile in California, many seem to have sensed this immense vitality. Quite correctly, too: for, contrary to the much-quoted assurance at the conclusion of *In the Jungle of Cities,* chaos, "the best of all times," was in Brecht's view never completely "used up." His impulsive desire to savor the orgiastic frenzy of the world and his delight in evoking images of it was, in fact, slowly sublimated to an unquenchable "curiosity about people," which, however, still persisted as desire, as a lust for life. Knowing that the thirst for pleasure is one of the greatest human virtues, as he paradoxically formulated it, Brecht never tired of indulging contentedly in the manifold pleasures of existence, the sensual as well as the intellectual. He praised whatever gives pleasure and thereby happiness. Baseness was no less important to him than the sublime. He praised the elegance of mathematical reasoning, the appreciative, critical sampling of a work of art, even the "joy of doubting." On the other hand, he praised girls' breasts; fresh, fragrant bread; goat cheese; beer; and the Finnish berry "plucked from the gray branch when the early dew falls." Brecht did not advocate indiscriminate guzzling, but rather an alert, sensitive, ever-increasing capacity for enjoyment, a quality that fills the spiritual sphere with solid sensuality and transfigures sensuality spiritually. In such pleasurable savoring of enjoyment—for "to create art is pleasurable"—Brecht's experience of life appears in its most sublimated form.

This basic experience engendered a group of fundamental types that can be traced through all of Brecht's works. The first of these incorporates the myth of an uninhibited thirst for existence: that is, the figure of Baal in Brecht's first play of the same name, written between 1918 and 1919. Imbibing, stuffing himself, whoring, and singing dirty songs, Baal goes reeling through the "eternal forest" until its dark womb pulls him down. Galileo and the fat Ziffel from the *Refugee Dialogues* also show traces of Baal's imprint. "I value the consolations of the flesh," admits the Florentine; "I say: To enjoy yourself is an achievement." For his part, Ziffel expounds on the advantages of the thirst for pleasure, believing in its moral value:

> I have often wondered why leftist writers do not use juicy descriptions of human pleasures for the purpose of political agitation.... I always see only handbooks that inform us about the philosophy and morals of the upper class. Why are there no handbooks about eating to one's heart's content and the other comforts and conveniences that lower-class people never enjoy? As though the only thing missing in the lives of the lower class were Kant! It's really sad that some people have never seen the pyramids of Egypt, but I find it even more oppressive that some people have never seen a filet in mushroom sauce. A simple description of the various types of cheese, palpably and vividly written, or an artistically conceived image of an authentic omelette would no doubt have a very educational effect.

Other figures personify not so much the enjoyment of life as its indestructibility. Highly significant in that respect is Brecht's first and most famous collection of poems, his *Hauspostille* ("Domestic Breviary") of 1927, to which was appended a plate showing a "water-fire-man," drawn by Brecht's friend Caspar Neher. This *hydatopyranthropus* apparently is meant to illustrate the new species of man that is alone able to survive in the asphalt jungles, "which are burning below and already freezing on top." The cunning, sensual survival artists that Brecht created later on are basically the same sort of indestructible elemental beings. All of them—Schweyk, Herr Keuner, or Azdak in *The Caucasian Chalk Circle* of 1945—last longer than power. Partially by instinct, partially by persistent slyness, they adapt to all situations and, like Ziffel and Galileo, steadfastly refuse to become heroes. "I don't have a backbone to crush," explains Herr Keuner. Only the Chinese God of Happiness, about whom Brecht and the composer Paul Dessau wanted to write an opera in the 1940s, could have become a hero. Unfortunately, this work remained only a sketch. But in 1954, in the preface to the new edition of his early plays, Brecht gave at least an outline of the story. The short, fat, luxuriating god of "taste buds and testicles" comes, according to Brecht, after a great war to find the ruined cities, and incites the people to "fight for their personal happiness and well-being." Arrested by the authorities and condemned to death, he resists all the arts of the executioners: he likes the taste of the poisons they give him; they cut off his head and it grows back; at the gallows, he performs a catchy, happy dance; and so on and so forth. "It is impossible to destroy completely man's desire for happiness," the poet summarizes. In other words, the God of Happiness, too, is an indestructible elemental being, a water-fire-man. One thing has changed since the 1920s, however. "Happiness is: Communism," Brecht said to Dessau. The poet wishes to legitimize the barbaric triumph of senseless life and naked, blindly proliferating greed on the basis of socialism and ethics, and thereby achieve direction and meaning; egoism, materialism, and Marxism are to be identical.

Hence, Brecht argued that human pleasures and desires are essentially good and are to be promoted. What transforms them into their opposite is simply the jungle law of capitalistic society, which forces man to become either a beast of prey or a neighing clod of flesh. This insight and the conclusion to which it leads—namely, that human happiness can only be attained by overthrowing the existing social order—describes the second basic experience that shaped Brecht's life. Retaining our terminology, it is Brecht's decisive educational experience *(Bildungserlebnis)* as opposed to his primal experience, or *Urerlebnis.* Contradictions, though, are certainly not lacking here. It was no accident that Brecht, three years before his death, was reluctantly forced to admit to himself that only the "tiger" qualified as an "artist of life." Verses written in exile reveal to what extent the fascination of chaos had remained alive within him: in these verses, the poet of class struggle voices his anxious concern that the sight of "so multifarious a world" could again meet with his "approval," with "pleasure at the contradictions of such a bloody life, you understand." By equating the desire for personal happiness of the individual with the fight for Communism, Brecht only covered over a dichotomy that in other instances had broken open all the more painfully.

As early as October 1926, Brecht began to lean toward Communism. At that time, the poet procured writings on socialism and Marxism, and asked for advice about which basic works he should study first. Shortly after, he wrote to his assistant Elisabeth Hauptmann: "I am eight feet deep in *Das Kapital.* I have to know this now exactly." Brecht, "thirsting for knowledge," and "searching through the years" for a model, as he himself wrote, had finally found what he needed. Full of eagerness and passion, he dedicated himself to this new experience. He demanded complete Marxism— not, as he mockingly put it in his *Refugee Dialogues,* "inferior" Marxism without Hegel or Ricardo. Brecht really wanted to "know it exactly." Thus, it is not unreasonable to compare his intensive study of Marxism with Schiller's lengthy study of Kant. Granted, the fact that the poet's first Marxist teachers, Fritz Sternberg and Karl Korsch, happened to be Communist heretics is not lacking in irony; yet it has an inner justification all the same. For Brecht the artist always remained, so to speak, a self-made Communist. Significantly, he never belonged to the party.

But just for that reason, we must be careful not to explain away Brecht's acceptance of Communism too quickly or easily. It is impossible to force the poet into the Procrustean bed of a simple psychological mechanism, as Martin Esslin tried to do. The motives which impelled Brecht were diverse. We have already spoken of his elemental "desire for pleasure" and the unrestricted intellectual curiosity that filled him. Artistic and philosophical considerations also play a part. Moreover, a certain predilection of the artist for the common people cannot be overlooked, either. In the "lower classes" and their struggles, the unaffiliated poet found the only thing with which he could "fully identify." Last but surely not least, experiences like that of May 1, 1929, when the Berlin police shot recklessly at peacefully demonstrating workers, and over twenty people died, seem finally to have decided the issue for him.

Toward the end of his life, Bertolt Brecht described his motives for embracing Marxism in the following words: "At certain times in history, social classes struggle for the leadership of humanity, and the desire to be among the pioneers and forge ahead is very strong in those who are not completely degenerate." Brecht's partiality for the "lesser folk" had three roots: history, moral discernment, and spontaneous feeling. It is evident that this threesome, in reverse order, reflects exactly the connection between the two decisive experiences of the poet. What once appeared as an immutable world order now appears under the guise of historical evolution. No longer is the fate of humanity determined by an unknowable "attitude of this planet," which man cannot influence, but by the state of society, created by man and therefore alterable by man. The "almost absolute determinism in which the young Brecht must have believed yields to the conviction that "man's fate is man." In consequence, for him, the born "describer of the world and behaviorist," it was only a step from this point to the insight that the struggles of humankind take the form of class struggles.

This altered experience of the world also expresses itself in almost compulsively recurring images. Two of them are especially meaningful. According to whether examined in an ethical or historical aspect, original chaos—the primeval forest, the thicket, the jungle—becomes a "hell" or a "deluge." The transition occurs slowly. For instance, in the opera *Rise and Fall of the City of Mahagonny,* a work that protests sharply against the "chaotic conditions of our cities" and the "unjust distribution of earthly possessions," God suddenly appears in an interlude and condemns the drunken men to Hell. They answer:

> Everyone's striking. By our hair
> You can't drag us down to Hell
> Because we've always been there.

Nevertheless, this work, written in 1928/29, ends with the bleak insight: "We can't help ourselves or you or anyone." Later works, on the other hand, such as *St. Joan of the Stockyards* (1929/30) or *The Good Woman of Sezuan* (1938/42), use the image of Hell in a completely Marxist manner. And Brecht treats the image of the Flood in exactly the same way: namely, at first in general terms, as a natural or historical catastrophe; finally, though, it clearly "breaks into the bourgeois world." As he phrased it: "First, there is still land, but with puddles that are turning into ponds and straits; then, there is only the dark water far and wide, with islands that quickly crumble."

Both conceptions (as well as the image of "paradise" for the promised new world) are biblical in origin. This is no coincidence. We know that Brecht answered an inquiry as to what had made the deepest impression on him with the statement: "You will laugh: the Bible." It is less-well known that the fifteen-year-old Brecht wrote a play on this very theme. The play was "published" in the mimeographed Augsburg student magazine *The Harvest* in January 1914. *The Bible,* a short, six-and-a-half page one-act play, deals with nothing less than the imitation of Christ. A city in the Netherlands is under siege during the religious wars, and is threatened with destruction. The mayor's daughter could save the city if she would yield herself up to the enemy captain. She is willing to sacrifice herself, but her grandfather's legalistic rigorism forbids it. His self-righteousness wins out over the Cross. For a fifteen-year-old, to choose such a theme and work it out, however awkwardly, is a sign of poetic genius, but even more strikingly, an indication of the hold that Christian teachings had upon him.

As a friend of Brecht's tells us: "In his youth, at any rate, [he] hardly rejected the core of Christianity; he attacked what he perceived to be its falsification." A scene in *The Caucasian Chalk Circle,* showing the maid Grusha before the helpless child of the deposed governor, indicates what this genuine spirit of Christianity actually meant to Brecht. The poet could not possibly have overlooked the fact that the parable of the Good Samaritan is reiterated here. How else could he have written those moving lines, the conclusion of which is so foreign to a piece conceived as a celebration of two Soviet collective farms? Just listen:

> Consider, woman, that one who does not hear a cry for help
> But passes by with distracted ear will never
> Hear again the hushed call of her lover nor
> The blackbird in the dawn nor the contented
> Sighs of the tired grape pickers at Angelus.

This natural morality was for Brecht the essence of Christianity. He called it *friendliness,* also *kindness,* but the proximity of such "words of the heart" *(Herzworte)* to Christian charity is unmistakable.

Otherwise, Brecht admittedly rejected the Christian heritage with scorn. Two of its traits enraged him most: the belief in a hereafter, and the church as an institution. Baptized and confirmed as a Protestant, he soon proceeded to demolish "the bourgeois belief in God." Brecht was not so much concerned with the existence of God as with the effect of belief in God on humanity. The poet weighed the value of God, as it were. For instance, his Herr Keuner answers the question about the existence of such a Being as follows:

> I advise you to reflect whether, depending upon the answer to this question, your behavior would alter. If it would not, we can drop the question. If it would, then at least I can be of some help to you by telling you that your mind is already made up: you need a God.

Brecht himself no longer needed God. Explaining that he had no feeling whatsoever for metaphysics, he was convinced, along with Karl Marx, that the abolition of religion as the source of the illusory happiness of humankind was a necessary condition for true happiness.

Later on, Brecht's vital desire to abolish religion and to make happiness materialize in this world changes more and more into an ethical postulate. The wild rejoicing above the abyss is muted: the poet is now holding a trial. One of his most shattering accusations calling Christianity to account on the basis of its own spirit of charity is the parable play *The Good Woman of Sezuan,* the content of which, seemingly so Eastern, is in reality based on the story of Sodom and Gomorrah. Brecht's reference to the fiery hail is unmistakable. Just as Lot receives the two angels of the Lord, so does the poor prostitute Shen Te receive the three wandering Chinese gods. But whereas in the Bible and in Brecht's like-named youthful play the town is actually destroyed by fire, the ending of *The Good Woman of Sezuan* is entirely different. No longer does God judge the world, which is Hell anyhow, but the world judges God. Since God (Who owes the good people a good world, as Shen Te sings) has organized His world so badly that even the best in it cannot be good, He is sentenced by the poet and condemned to nothingness. The scene in Brecht's parable play becomes a deadly tribunal, from which the three "illuminated ones" can extricate themselves only by means of a ridiculous ascension to Heaven—the very opposite of the deus ex machina solution.

This ambivalent relationship to Christianity is a hidden impulse that led to the poet's acceptance of Marxism. Without it, Brecht's encounter with Communism would never have attained its vital meaning. Precisely his Marxist inclinations, however, which Brecht felt had taught him absolute knowledge and perfectibility of the world, inevitably involved him from the start in tragedy. It manifested itself as an incurable dichotomy between the desire for personal happiness of the individual and the fight for Communism. Brecht realized, along with Shen Te:

> To let none be destroyed, not even oneself
> To bring happiness to all, including oneself
> Is good.

But the attempt at transforming the categorical imperative of materialism into action not only split the good woman of Sezuan "like a lightning bolt in two," but even more so the poet. Shen Te cannot be good since she lives in a world where no one can be good. Bertolt Brecht cannot be good because he fights for a world where everyone can finally be good—yet the road to this Paradise is through Hell.

Brecht the Marxist was faced with a terrible choice. In demanding the complete humanization of humankind—in which he believed—he was forced either to require also its complete dehumanization and objectification, or else to question the ideology itself, the highest value of his life and work. Indeed, he might even be faced with the necessity of negating this ideology. That schism comes to the fore most painfully in Brecht's didactic play *The Measures Taken,* which, unbeknownst to the poet, evolved into a tragedy. It tells how four Communist agitators shoot one of their fellow fighters and throw him into a lime pit. This young comrade embodies natural morality, immediate succor here and now; the agitators embody ideology, the future and all-encompassing salvation of mankind. If the Marxist classics (i.e., Marx, Engels, and Lenin) do not concede that every individual is to be helped "at once and before everything else," then, shouts the young comrade, they are "dirt" *(Dreck).* And he goes on: "I tear them up. For man, living man, cries out. His misery tears down the dikes of mere teaching." The agitators, on the other hand, "empty pages" upon which "the Revolution writes its directions," have stifled all spontaneous human feelings within themselves, and their sinister maxim is:

> What baseness would you not commit
> To root out baseness?

Such, if anything, are the ineluctable constraints of end and means.

Brecht could only cover over but not resolve this tragic dichotomy between ideology and natural morality. The Marxist poet must necessarily wish for both yet desire neither. Thus, in *The Measures Taken,* he decided in favor of the agitators and their "bloody hands," but he banned all subsequent presentations of the play; and whereas he never tired of warning against pity and of making fun of self-sacrifice, he created touching female characters who not only take pity on their fellow humans but are even prepared to die for them, like Mute Kattrin in *Mother Courage and Her Children.* Only twice more, so it seems, did the poet express his profound misgivings about the highest value of his existence: during the infamous Stalinist purges and after the events of June 17, 1953, the workers' uprising crushed by Russian tanks. One of the so-called *Buckow Elegies,* written at that time, ends with the lines:

> Last night in a dream I saw fingers pointing at me
> As a leper. They were worn with toil and
> They were broken.
>
> You don't know! I shrieked
> Conscience-stricken.

Did Bertolt Brecht, composing these lines, think also of the First of May, 1929? What might he have felt?

But Brecht shifted his glance from the Gorgonian visage of tragedy. He did not want to perceive it. Another poem from his later years reads:

> Don't believe your eyes
> Don't believe your ears.
> What you see is darkness.
> Perhaps it is light.

Instead of insisting on utter doubt and, in the long run, despair, Brecht accepted the ignominy of coming to terms with the frailty of his world. He upheld the final humanization of humankind but still followed the humanitarian insight that this goal was not worth any more than the way that leads to it. What remained, however, was not only hope dampened by resignation, but primarily the ability, derived from that basic experience of the poet, to make "dialectics a pleasure" for himself and for others. As early as 1920, Brecht admitted his "enjoyment of pure dialectics." Accordingly, and even in his posthumous writings, he extolled the surprises of evolution, the instability of the human condition, and the humor in contradictoriness. "Those are pleasures in the vitality of human beings, things, and processes," he said, "and they enhance both the art and the joy of living." Quite rightly, the poet has been called a habitual, indeed constitutional, Hegelian. Just as alienation, as a dialectic manifestation of contradictions, represents the basic principle of his creativity, so dialectics, as a teaching and experience of the eternally changing "flow of becoming," represents the basic principle of his life and thought. It also determines Brecht's position in history. As he declared: "In times of revolution [*Umwälzungen*]—the fearsome and fruitful ones [*die furchtbaren und fruchtbaren*]—the evenings of the declining classes merge with the mornings of the rising classes. Those are the periods of twilight in which the owl of Minerva begins its flights." What is elevated here into the mature lucidity of the famous dictum of Hegel's, once poured itself out as a chaotic flood in verses like this:

> He has a longing in him: for death by drowning
> And he has a longing in him: not to go down.

(In both instances, it should be noted, Brecht employs the word *Lust,* near synonymous here with *Wollust,* or its English equivalent, "lust.")

If one connects these two testimonies, one will be able to grasp the contradictory unity that supported the life, and the feeling for life, of this man. For Bertolt Brecht was always a poet of transition, the changing and changeable interlude of the No Longer and the

Not Yet. "Descendant" and "ancestor" at the same time, he lived, for all his intensity, "without [a real] present"—so that one might almost be tempted to designate his exile, in which he remained for fifteen years, as his actual home, or even as an image of his whole existence. Not by chance did Brecht choose the mask of his cunning Herr Keuner. This Swabian "no one" *(keiner)* can be traced right down to the Homeric wanderer Ulysses, the first to adopt the name of Οὖτις, or "no one."

Moreover, and finally—art. It must be obvious that a poet like Brecht could never regard it as something hermetic or static. Considering those solutions the best, which in turn create new problems, he loved anything that was open, changing, evolving, dynamic—indeed extending to the paradoxical consequence that one should make a habit of preventing "anything from being finished." Even objects of art are inundated by the flood of becoming. They are not marked by any formalistic perfection, but by an animated, ever renewed exchange:

> Half ruined buildings once again take on
> The look of buildings waiting to be finished
> Generously planned: their fine proportions
> Can already be guessed at, but they still
> Need our understanding. At the same time
> They have already served, already been overcome. All this
> Delights me.

Dies alles / Beglückt mich. Art and life permeate one another. "All arts," so said the poet, "contribute to the greatest of all arts: the art of living." They increase the joy of living, and the joy of living is identical, as it were, with the desire to change oneself.

> Everything changes. You can make
> A fresh start with your final breath.

This was Bertolt Brecht's legacy.

* * *

So much then, however sketchy, for a portrayal of Brecht's life and work. Thus, can he, the self-proclaimed classical author of long standing, in truth be ranked as a modern classic? Yet what is classical anyhow? According to Shipley's *Dictionary of World Literature,* a classical oeuvre is one that "merits lasting interest," being "marked by individuality and universality." That, I am afraid, reveals itself as all too vague, all too trite and hackneyed. Gero von Wilpert, in his German counterpart, *Sachwörterbuch der Literatur,* offers a more concise, more concrete definition. According to him, modern classics are first-rate modern authors in general and, in particular, authors who have been seminal, nay exemplary, within the realm of a certain genre. Surely, Brecht qualifies on all those counts. Most impressively, he has proved himself a preeminent figure in modern literature: his influence is felt worldwide. Doubtless, his dramatic impact, after its early phases in the German-speaking community and, subsequently, all over Europe in the 1950s, has meanwhile spread across the globe, and notably the entire Third World. It is equally manifest in the work of the Nigerian Nobel Prize laureate Wole Soyinka, the pieces of the Argentine playwright Osvaldo Dragún, or the guerilla theater in the remote villages of the Philippines—to cite but three examples. A consummate master of overall theatrical theory and practice, Brecht has likewise been the creator of a classical (and now almost canonical) form of modern drama and theater: to wit, its epic, non–Aristotelian brand imbued with distance and alienation.

In regard to the narrower confines of German literature, and its poetry especially, Brecht must be hailed as the propagator and unsurpassed master of what he labeled "rhymeless lyrics with irregular rhythm"—a kind of modern verse that has long since become the all-important, all-inclusive model of contemporary German poetry. And to top it all off, together with Goethe, Heine, and Nietzsche, Brecht must be recognized as one of the greatest innovators and/or renovators of German poetic speech derived, as in the case of those towering predecessors, from Martin Luther's translation of the Bible, the very wellspring of present-day German at large.

To my mind, there cannot be the slightest doubt that Bertolt Brecht is, and will remain, a genuine modern classic, just as Dante Alighieri, with whom I began, has been a genuine medieval one for so many centuries.

R.G.

Part 1
Poetry

Prelude

O LUST DES BEGINNENS

O Lust des Beginnens! O früher Morgen!
Erstes Gras, wenn vergessen scheint
Was grün ist! O erste Seite des Buchs
Des erwarteten, sehr überraschende! Lies
Langsam, allzuschnell
Wird der ungelesene Teil dir dünn! Und der erste Wasserguß
In das verschweißte Gesicht! Das frische
Kühle Hemd! O Beginn der Liebe! Blick, der wegirrt!
O Beginn der Arbeit! Öl zu füllen
In die kalte Maschine! Erster Handgriff und erstes Summen
Des anspringenden Motors! Und erster Zug
Rauchs, der die Lunge füllt! Und du
Neuer Gedanke!

ON THE JOY OF BEGINNING

Oh joy of beginning! Oh early morning!
First grass, when none remembers
What green looks like. Oh first page of the book
Long awaited, the surprise of it. Read it
Slowly, all too soon the unread part
Will be too thin for you. And the first splash of water
On a sweaty face! The fresh
Cool shirt. Oh the beginning of love! Glance that strays away!
Oh the beginning of work! Pouring oil
Into the cold machine. First touch and first hum
Of the engine springing to life! And first drag
Of smoke filling the lungs! And you too
New thought!

Translated by Humphrey Milnes

From *Bertolt Brecht's Domestic Breviary* (1927)

VON DER FREUNDLICHKEIT DER WELT

1
Auf die Erde voller kaltem Wind
Kamt ihr alle als ein nacktes Kind.
Frierend lagt ihr ohne alle Hab
Als ein Weib euch eine Windel gab.

2
Keiner schrie euch, ihr wart nicht begehrt
Und man holte euch nicht im Gefährt.
Hier auf Erden wart ihr unbekannt
Als ein Mann euch einst nahm an der Hand.

3
Von der Erde voller kaltem Wind
Geht ihr all bedeckt mit Schorf und Grind.
Fast ein jeder hat die Welt geliebt
Wenn man ihm zwei Hände Erde gibt.

GROßER DANKCHORAL

1
Lobet die Nacht und die Finsternis, die euch umfangen!
Kommet zuhauf
Schaut in den Himmel hinauf:
Schon ist der Tag euch vergangen.

2
Lobet das Gras und die Tiere, die neben euch leben und sterben!
Sehet, wie ihr
Lebet das Gras und das Tier
Und es muß auch mit euch sterben.

OF THE FRIENDLINESS OF THE WORLD

1
To this windy world of chill distress
You all came in utter nakedness
Cold you lay and destitute of all
Till a woman wrapped you in a shawl.

2
No one called you, none bade you approach
And you were not fetched by groom and coach.
Strangers were you in this early land
When a man once took you by the hand.

3
From this windy world of chill distress
You all part in rot and filthiness.
Almost everyone has loved the world
When on him two clods of earth are hurled.

Translated by Karl Neumann

GREAT HYMN OF THANKSGIVING

1
Worship the night and the darkness by which you're surrounded!
Come with a shove
Look to the heaven above:
Day is already confounded.

2
Worship the grass and the beasts that have life and must perish!
Lo! Grass and beasts
Like you partake of life's feasts
Like you they also must perish.

3
Lobet den Baum, der aus Aas aufwächst jauchzend zum Himmel!
Lobet das Aas
Lobet den Baum, der es fraß
Aber auch lobet den Himmel.

4
Lobet von Herzen das schlechte Gedächtnis des Himmels!
Und daß er nicht
Weiß euren Nam noch Gesicht
Niemand weiß, daß ihr noch da seid.

5
Lobet die Kälte, die Finsternis und das Verderben!
Schauet hinan:
Es kommet nicht auf euch an
Und ihr könnt unbesorgt sterben.

ERINNERUNG AN DIE MARIE A.

1
An jenem Tag im blauen Mond September
Still unter einem jungen Pflaumenbaum
Da hielt ich sie, die stille bleiche Liebe
In meinem Arm wie einen holden Traum.
Und über uns im schönen Sommerhimmel
War eine Wolke, die ich lange sah
Sie war sehr weiß und ungeheuer oben
Und als ich aufsah, war sie nimmer da.

2
Seit jenem Tag sind viele, viele Monde
Geschwommen still hinunter und vorbei.

3
Worship the tree that from carrion soars up towards heaven!
Worship the rot
Worship the tree it begot
But furthermore worship heaven.

4
Worship with fulness of heart the weak memory of heaven!
It cannot trace
Either your name or your face
Nobody knows you're still living.

5
Worship the cold and the dark and calamity dire!
Scan the whole earth:
You're a thing of no worth
And you may calmly expire.

Translated by Karl Neumann

REMEMBERING MARIE A.

It was a day in that blue month September
Silent beneath a plum tree's slender shade
I held her there, my love so pale and silent
As if she were a dream that must not fade.
Above us in the shining summer heaven
There was a cloud my eyes dwelt long upon
It was quite white and very high above us
Then I looked up, and found that it had gone.

And since that day so many moons, in silence
Have swum across the sky and gone below.
The plum trees surely have been chopped for firewood
And if you ask, how does that love seem now?

Die Pflaumenbäume sind wohl abgehauen
Und fragst du mich, was mit der Liebe sei?
So sag ich dir: ich kann mich nicht erinnern.
Und doch, gewiß, ich weiß schon, was du meinst
Doch ihr Gesicht, das weiß ich wirklich nimmer
Ich weiß nur mehr: ich küßte es dereinst.

3
Und auch den Kuß, ich hätt ihn längst vergessen
Wenn nicht die Wolke dagewesen wär
Die weiß ich noch und werd ich immer wissen
Sie war sehr weiß und kam von oben her.
Die Pflaumenbäume blühn vielleicht noch immer
Und jene Frau hat jetzt vielleicht das siebte Kind
Doch jene Wolke blühte nur Minuten
Und als ich aufsah, schwand sie schon im Wind.

BALLADE VON DER HANNA CASH

1
Mit dem Rock von Kattun und dem gelben Tuch
Und den Augen der schwarzen Seen
Ohne Geld und Talent und doch mit genug
Vom Schwarzhaar, das sie offen trug
Bis zu den schwärzeren Zeh'n:
Das war die Hanna Cash, mein Kind
Die die »Gentlemen« eingeseift
Die kam mit dem Wind und ging mit dem Wind
Der in die Savannen läuft.

2
Die hatte keine Schuhe und die hatte auch kein Hemd
Und die konnte auch keine Choräle!
Und sie war wie eine Katze in die große Stadt geschwemmt

I must admit: I really can't remember
And yet I know what you are trying to say.
But what her face was like I know no longer
I only know: I kissed it on that day.

As for the kiss, I'd long ago forgot it
But for the cloud that floated in the sky
I know that still, and shall for ever know it
It was quite white and moved in very high.
It may be that the plum trees still are blooming
That woman's seventh child may now be there
And yet that cloud had only bloomed for minutes
When I looked up, it vanished on the air.

Translated by John Willett

BALLAD OF HANNAH CASH

1
With her thin cotton skirt and her yellow shawl
And her eyes twin pools of jet
And no talent or money, she still had it all
From her hair like a clear black waterfall
To her toes that were blacker yet:
*Yes, that was Hannah Cash, my friend
Who made the toffs pay through the nose.
With the wind she came and with the wind she went
As across the savannahs it blows.*

2
She hadn't a blouse and she hadn't a hat
As for hymns to sing, she had still fewer.
She washed into the city like a half-drowned cat

Eine kleine graue Katze zwischen Hölzer eingeklemmt
Zwischen Leichen in die schwarzen Kanäle.
Sie wusch die Gläser vom Absinth
Doch nie sich selber rein
Und doch muß die Hanna Cash, mein Kind
Auch rein gewesen sein.

3
Und sie kam eines Nachts in die Seemannsbar
Mit den Augen der schwarzen Seen
Und traf J. Kent mit dem Maulwurfshaar
Den Messerjack aus der Seemannsbar
Und der ließ sie mit sich gehn!
Und wenn der wüste Kent den Grind
Sich kratzte und blinzelte
Dann spürt die Hanna Cash, mein Kind
Den Blick bis in die Zeh.

4
Sie »kamen sich näher« zwischen Wild und Fisch
Und »gingen vereint durchs Leben«
Sie hatten kein Bett und sie hatten keinen Tisch
Und sie hatten selber nicht Wild noch Fisch
Und keinen Namen für die Kinder.
Doch ob Schneewind pfeift, ob Regen rinnt
Ersöff auch die Savann
Es bleibt die Hanna Cash, mein Kind
Bei ihrem lieben Mann.

5
Der Sheriff sagt, daß er ein Schurke sei
Und die Milchfrau sagt: er geht krumm.
Sie aber sagt: Was ist dabei?
Es ist mein Mann. Und sie war so frei
Und blieb bei ihm. Darum.

A little grey creature that clawed and spat
Thrust with corpses in a black sewer.
> *She washed the glasses clean of absinthe*
> *Herself she never got clean*
> *You ask, was Hannah Cash pure, my friend?*
> *I'd say she must have been.*

3
One night she went to the Sailors' Bar
With her eyes twin pools of jet
And found J. Kent of the moleskin hair—
Yes, Slasher Jack from the Sailors' Bar
Who took what he could get.
> *Straightway Kent's eyes began to flash*
> *As he picked his scabby nose:*
> *Those eyes, my friend, shook Hannah Cash*
> *Right down to the tip of her toes.*

4
They "found common ground" between fish and game
And it made them "companions for life"
They themselves had no table, no fish or game
They hadn't a bed, nor had they a name
For any children who might arrive.
> *The blizzards can howl, it can rain without end*
> *The savannah can flood far and wide*
> *But Hannah Cash's place, my friend*
> *Is by her husband's side.*

5
The milk woman says he can't walk erect
The sheriff calls him a rat.
But Hannah says: you are correct
He is my man. If you don't object
I'll stick by him. Because of that.

Und wenn er hinkt und wenn er spinnt
Und wenn er ihr Schläge gibt:
Es fragt die Hanna Cash, mein Kind
Doch nur: ob sie ihn liebt.

6
Kein Dach war da, wo die Wiege war
Und die Schläge schlugen die Eltern.
Die gingen zusammen Jahr für Jahr
Aus der Asphaltstadt in die Wälder gar
Und in die Savann aus den Wäldern.
Solang man geht in Schnee und Wind
Bis daß man nicht mehr kann
So lang ging die Hanna Cash, mein Kind
Nun mal mit ihrem Mann.

7
Kein Kleid war arm, wie das ihre war
Und es gab keinen Sonntag für sie
Keinen Ausflug zu dritt in die Kirschtortenbar
Und keinen Weizenfladen im Kar
Und keine Mundharmonie.
Und war jeder Tag, wie alle sind
Und gab's kein Sonnenlicht:
Es hatte die Hanna Cash, mein Kind
Die Sonn stets im Gesicht.

8
Er stahl wohl die Fische, und Salz stahl sie.
So war's. »Das Leben ist schwer.«
Und wenn sie die Fische kochte, sieh:
So sagten die Kinder auf seinem Knie
Den Katechismus her.
Durch fünfzig Jahr in Nacht und Wind
Sie schliefen in einem Bett.

He may be lame, he may be mad
He may beat her as he will:
All that worries Hannah Cash, my lad
Is—does she love him still?

6
No roof above the cot was there
Nothing mild in the parents' manners.
Never apart, year after year
From the city to the forests went that pair
From the forests to the savannahs.
    When winds are cold and blizzards wild
    You keep moving as long as you can.
    So long did Hannah Cash, my child
    Move onwards with her man.

7
No one so poorly dressed as she
She never had a Sunday fling
No trips to pastrycooks for tea
No wheaten cakes in Lent for three
No choir in which to sing.
    And every day might be as sad
    As every other one:
    On the darkest days Hannah Cash, my lad
    Was always bathed in sun.

8
She stole the salt, the fishes he.
That's all. Such heroism.
And as she cooks those fishes, see
The children sitting on his knee
Learning their catechism.
    Through fifty years of night and wind
    They shared each other's bed.

Das war die Hanna Cash, mein Kind
Gott mach's ihr einmal wett.

VON DER KINDESMÖRDERIN MARIE FARRAR

1
Marie Farrar, geboren im April
Unmündig, merkmallos, rachitisch, Waise
Bislang angeblich unbescholten, will
Ein Kind ermordet haben in der Weise:
Sie sagt, sie habe schon im zweiten Monat
Bei einer Frau in einem Kellerhaus
Versucht, es abzutreiben mit zwei Spritzen
Angeblich schmerzhaft, doch ging's nicht heraus.
Doch ihr, ich bitte euch, wollt nicht in Zorn verfallen
Denn alle Kreatur braucht Hilf von allen.

2
Sie habe dennoch, sagt sie, gleich bezahlt
Was ausgemacht war, sich fortan geschnürt
Auch Sprit getrunken, Pfeffer drin vermahlt
Doch habe sie das nur stark abgeführt.
Ihr Leib sei zusehends geschwollen, habe
Auch stark geschmerzt, beim Tellerwaschen oft.
Sie selbst sei, sagt sie, damals noch gewachsen.
Sie habe zu Marie gebetet, viel erhofft.
Auch ihr, ich bitte euch, wollt nicht in Zorn verfallen
Denn alle Kreatur braucht Hilf von allen.

3
Doch die Gebete hätten, scheinbar, nichts genützt.
Es war auch viel verlangt. Als sie dann dicker war
Hab ihr in Frühmetten geschwindelt. Oft hab sie geschwitzt

Yes, that was Hannah Cash, my friend
God rest her weary head.

Translated by John Willett

ON THE INFANTICIDE MARIE FARRAR

1

Marie Farrar: month of birth, April
An orphaned minor; rickets; birthmarks, none; previously
Of good character, admits that she did kill
Her child as follows here in summary.
She visited a woman in a basement
During her second month, so she reported
And there was given two injections
Which, though they hurt, did not abort it.
   But you I beg, make not your anger manifest
   For all that lives needs help from all the rest.

2

But nonetheless, she says, she paid the bill
As was arranged, then bought herself a corset
And drank neat spirit, peppered it as well
But that just made her vomit and disgorge it.
Her belly now was noticeably swollen
And ached when she washed up the plates.
She says that she had not finished growing.
She prayed to Mary, and her hopes were great.
   You too I beg, make not your anger manifest
   For all that lives needs help from all the rest.

3

Her prayers, however, seemed to be no good.
She'd asked too much. Her belly swelled. At Mass
She started to feel dizzy and she would

Auch Angstschweiß, häufig unter dem Altar.
Doch hab den Zustand sie geheim gehalten
Bis die Geburt sie nachher überfiel.
Es sei gegangen, da wohl niemand glaubte
Daß sie, sehr reizlos, in Versuchung fiel.
Und ihr, ich bitte euch, wollt nicht in Zorn verfallen
Denn alle Kreatur braucht Hilf von allen.

4
An diesem Tag, sagt sie, in aller Früh
Ist ihr beim Stiegenwischen so, als krallten
Ihr Nägel in den Bauch. Es schüttelt sie.
Jedoch gelingt es ihr, den Schmerz geheimzuhalten.
Den ganzen Tag, es ist beim Wäschehängen
Zerbricht sie sich den Kopf; dann kommt sie drauf
Daß sie gebären sollte, und es wird ihr
Gleich schwer ums Herz. Erst spät geht sie hinauf.
Doch ihr, ich bitte euch, wollt nicht in Zorn verfallen
Denn alle Kreatur braucht Hilf von allen.

5
Man holte sie noch einmal, als sie lag:
Schnee war gefallen und sie mußte kehren.
Das ging bis elf. Es war ein langer Tag.
Erst in der Nacht konnte sie in Ruhe gebären.
Und sie gebar, so sagt sie, einen Sohn.
Der Sohn war ebenso wie andere Söhne.
Doch sie war nicht so wie die anderen, obschon:
Es liegt kein Grund vor, daß ich sie verhöhne.
Auch ihr, ich bitte euch, wollt nicht in Zorn verfallen
Denn alle Kreatur braucht Hilf von allen.

6
So will ich also weiter denn erzählen
Wie es mit diesem Sohn geworden ist
(Sie wollte davon, sagt sie, nichts verhehlen)

Kneel in a cold sweat before the Cross.
Still she contrived to keep her true state hidden
Until the hour of birth itself was on her
Being so plain that no one could imagine
That any man would ever want to tempt her.
> *But you I beg, make not your anger manifest*
> *For all that lives needs help from all the rest.*

4

She says that on the morning of that day
While she was scrubbing stairs, something came clawing
Into her guts. It shook her once and went away.
She managed to conceal her pain and keep from crying.
As she, throughout the day, hung up the washing
She racked her brain, then realised in fright
She was going to give birth. At once a crushing
Weight grabbed at her heart. She didn't go upstairs till night.
> *And yet I beg, make not your anger manifest*
> *For all that lives needs help from all the rest.*

5

But just as she lay down they fetched her back again:
Fresh snow had fallen, and it must be swept.
That was a long day. She worked till after ten.
She could not give birth in peace till the household slept.
And then she bore, so she reports, a son.
The son was like the son of any mother.
But she was not like other mothers are—but then
There are no valid grounds why I should mock her.
> *You too I beg, make not your anger manifest*
> *For all that lives needs help from all the rest.*

6

So let her finish now and end her tale
About what happened to the son she bore
(She says there's nothing she will not reveal)

Damit man sieht, wie ich bin und du bist.
Sie sagt, sie sei, nur kurz im Bett, von Übel-
keit stark befallen worden und, allein
Hab sie, nicht wissend, was geschehen sollte
Mit Mühe sich bezwungen, nicht zu schrein.
Und ihr, ich bitte euch, wollt nicht in Zorn verfallen
Denn alle Kreatur braucht Hilf von allen.

7
Mit letzter Kraft hab sie, so sagt sie, dann
Da ihre Kammer auch eiskalt gewesen
Sich zum Abort geschleppt und dort auch (wann
Weiß sie nicht mehr) geborn ohn Federlesen
So gegen Morgen. Sie sei, sagt sie
Jetzt ganz verwirrt gewesen, habe dann
Halb schon erstarrt, das Kind kaum halten können
Weil es in den Gesindabort hereinschnein kann.
Auch ihr, ich bitte euch, wollt nicht in Zorn verfallen
Denn alle Kreatur braucht Hilf von allen.

8
Dann zwischen Kammer und Abort, vorher sagt sie
Sei noch gar nichts gewesen, fing das Kind
Zu schreien an, das hab sie so verdrossen, sagt sie
Daß sie's mit beiden Fäusten ohne Aufhörn, blind
So lang geschlagen habe, bis es still war, sagt sie.
Hierauf hab sie das Tote noch gradaus
Zu sich ins Bett genommen für den Rest der Nacht
Und es versteckt am Morgen in dem Wäschehaus.
Doch ihr, ich bitte euch, wollt nicht in Zorn verfallen
Denn alle Kreatur braucht Hilf vor allem.

9
Marie Farrar, geboren im April
Gestorben im Gefängnishaus zu Meißen
Ledige Kindesmutter, abgeurteilt, will

So men may see what I am and you are.
She'd just climbed into bed, she says, when nausea
Seized her. Never knowing what should happen till
It did, she struggled with herself to hush her
Cries, and forced them down. The room was still.
And you I beg, make not your anger manifest
For all that lives needs help from all the rest.

7
The bedroom was ice cold, so she called on
Her last remaining strength and dragged her-
Self out to the privy and there, near dawn
Unceremoniously, she was delivered
(Exactly when, she doesn't know). Then she
Now totally confused, she says, half froze
And found that she could scarcely hold the child
For the servants' privy lets in the heavy snows.
And you I beg, make not your anger manifest
For all that lives needs help from all the rest.

8
Between the servants' privy and her bed (she says
That nothing happened until then), the child
Began to cry, which vexed her so, she says
She beat it with her fists, hammering blind and wild
Without a pause until the child was quiet, she says.
She took the baby's body into bed
And held it for the rest of the night, she says
Then in the morning hid it in the laundry shed.
But you I beg, make not your anger manifest
For all that lives needs help from all the rest.

9
Marie Farrar: month of birth, April
Died in the Meissen penitentiary
An unwed mother, judged by the law, she will

Euch die Gebrechen aller Kreatur erweisen.
Ihr, die ihr gut gebärt in saubern Wochenbetten
Und nennt »gesegnet« euren schwangeren Schoß
Wollt nicht verdammen die verworfnen Schwachen
Denn ihre Sünd war schwer, doch ihr Leid groß.
Darum, ich bitte euch, wollt nicht in Zorn verfallen
Denn alle Kreatur braucht Hilf von allen.

GESANG DES SOLDATEN DER ROTEN ARMEE

1
Weil unser Land zerfressen ist
Mit einer matten Sonne drin
Spie es uns aus in dunkle Straßen
Und frierende Chausseen hin.

2
Schneewasser wusch im Frühjahr die Armee
Sie ist des roten Sommers Kind!
Schon im Oktober fiel auf sie der Schnee
Ihr Herz zerfror im Januarwind.

3
In diesen Jahren fiel das Wort Freiheit
Aus Mündern, drinnen Eis zerbrach.
Und viele sah man mit Tigergebissen
Ziehend der roten, unmenschlichen Fahne nach.

4
Oft abends, wenn im Hafer rot
Der Mond schwamm, vor dem Schlaf am Gaul
Redeten sie von kommenden Zeiten
Bis sie einschliefen, denn der Marsch macht faul.

Show you how all that lives, lives frailly.
You who bear your sons in laundered linen sheets
And call your pregnancies a "blessed" state
Should never damn the outcast and the weak:
Her sin was heavy, but her suffering great.
   Therefore, I beg, make not your anger manifest
   For all that lives needs help from all the rest.

Translated by Sidney H. Bremer

SONG OF THE SOLDIER OF THE RED ARMY

1
Because our land is eaten up
With an exhausted sun in it
It spat us out on to dark pavements
And country roads of frozen grit.

2
The melting slush washed the army in the spring
It was a child of summer's red.
Then in October snow began to fall
In January's winds its breast froze dead.

3
In those years talk of Freedom came
From lips inside which ice had cracked
And you saw many with jaws like tigers
Following the red, inhuman flag.

4
And when the moon swam red across the fields
Each resting on his horse's side
They often spoke about the times that were coming
Then fell asleep, made sluggish by the ride.

5
Im Regen und im dunklen Winde
War Schlaf uns schön auf hartem Stein.
Der Regen wusch die schmutzigen Augen
Von Schmutz und vielen Sünden rein.

6
Oft wurde nachts der Himmel rot
Sie hielten's für das Rot der Früh.
Dann war es Brand, doch auch das Frührot kam
Die Freiheit, Kinder, die kam nie.

7
Und drum: wo immer sie auch warn
Das ist die Hölle, sagten sie.
Die Zeit verging. Die letzte Hölle
War doch die allerletzte Hölle nie.

8
Sehr viele Höllen kamen noch.
Die Freiheit, Kinder, die kam nie.
Die Zeit vergeht. Doch kämen jetzt die Himmel
Die Himmel wären ohne sie.

9
Wenn unser Leib zerfressen ist
Mit einem matten Herzen drin
Speit die Armee einst unser Haut und Knochen
In kalte flache Löcher hin.

10
Und mit dem Leib, von Regen hart
Und mit dem Herz, versehrt von Eis
Und mit den blutbefleckten leeren Händen
So kommen wir grinsend in euer Paradeis.

5
In rain and in the murky wind
Hard stone seemed good to sleep upon.
The rain washed out our filthy eyes and cleansed them
Of filth and many a varied sin.

6
Often at night the sky turned red
They thought red dawn had come again.
That was a fire, but the dawn came also.
Freedom, my children, never came.

7
And so, wherever they might be
They looked around and said, it's hell.
The time went by. The latest hell, though
Was never the very last hell of all.

8
So many hells were still to come.
Freedom, my children, never came.
The time goes by. But if the heavens came now
Those heavens would be much the same.

9
When once our body's eaten up
With an exhausted heart in it
The army spews our skin and bones out
Into cold and shallow pits.

10
And with our body hard from rain
And with our heart all scarred by ice
And with our bloodstained empty hands we
Come grinning into your paradise.

Translated by John Willett

VON DES CORTEZ LEUTEN

Am siebten Tage unter leichten Winden
Wurden die Wiesen heller. Da die Sonne gut war
Gedachten sie zu rasten. Rollten Branntwein
Von ihren Wägen, machten Ochsen los.
Die schlachteten sie gegen Abend. Da es kühl wurd
Schlug man vom Holz des nachbarlichen Sumpfes
Armdicke Äste, knorrig, gut zu brennen.
Dann schlangen sie gewürztes Fleisch hinunter
Und fingen singend um die neunte Stunde
Mit Trinken an. Die Nacht war kühl und grün.
Mit heisrer Kehle, tüchtig vollgesogen
Mit einem letzten, kühlen Blick nach großen Sternen
Entschliefen sie gen Mitternacht am Feuer.
Sie schlafen schwer, doch mancher wußte morgens
Daß er die Ochsen einmal brüllen hörte.
Erwacht gen Mittag, sind sie schon im Wald.
Mit glasigen Augen, schweren Gliedern, heben
Sie ächzend sich aufs Knie und sehen staunend
Armdicke Äste, knorrig, um sie stehen
Höher als mannshoch, sehr verwirrt, mit Blattwerk
Und kleinen Blüten süßlichen Geruchs.
Es ist sehr schwül schon unter ihrem Dach
Das sich zu dichten scheint. Die heiße Sonne
Ist nicht zu sehen, auch der Himmel nicht.
Der Hauptmann brüllt als wie ein Stier nach Äxten.
Die liegen drüben, wo die Ochsen brüllten.
Man sieht sie nicht. Mit rauhen Flüchen stolpern
Die Leute im Geviert, ans Astwerk stoßend
Das zwischen ihnen durchgekrochen war.
Mit schlaffen Armen werfen sie sich wild
In die Gewächse, die leicht zittern, so
Als ginge leichter Wind von außen durch sie.
Nach Stunden Arbeit pressen sie die Stirnen
Schweißglänzend finster an die fremden Äste.

OF CORTEZ'S MEN

On the seventh day, when the winds were gentle
The meadows grew brighter. As the sun was good
They thought of resting. Rolled out brandy
From the waggons and unhitched some oxen.
They slaughtered them that evening. As it grew cooler
They hacked from timber in the marsh near by
Arm-thick branches, knotty, good for burning.
Then they set to devouring highly spiced meat
And about the ninth hour, singing
Began to drink. The night was cool and green.
Throats hoarsened, soundly soused and sated
With a last cool look at the big stars
They went to sleep by the fire towards midnight.
They slept deep, but many a one in the morning
Knew he'd heard the oxen bellow—once.
Waking at noon, they're already in the forest.
Glazed eyes, dull limbs, groaning
They hobble up and see in wonder
Arm-thick branches, knotty, all round them
Higher than a man, much tangled with foliage
And small sweet-smelling flowers.
It grows sultry under their roof; this
Seems to be thickening. The hot sun
Is not to be seen or the sky either.
The captain bellows like a bull for axes
But they're over there where the oxen are lowing.
Out of sight. Foully cursing, they stumble
About the camp, knocking against the branches
That have crept between them.
Arms slack, they hurl themselves wildly
Into the growth, which slightly shivers
As though stirred by a light breeze from outside it.
After hours of work gloomily they press their sweating
Foreheads against the alien branches.

Die Äste wuchsen und vermehrten langsam
Das schreckliche Gewirr. Später, am Abend
Der dunkler war, weil oben Blattwerk wuchs
Sitzen sie schweigend, angstvoll und wie Affen
In ihren Käfigen, von Hunger matt.
Nachts wuchs das Astwerk. Doch es mußte Mond sein
Es war noch ziemlich hell, sie sahn sich noch.
Erst gegen Morgen war das Zeug so dick
Daß sie sich nimmer sahen, bis sie starben.
Den nächsten Tag stieg Singen aus dem Wald.
Dumpf und verhallt. Sie sangen sich wohl zu.
Nachts ward es stiller. Auch die Ochsen schwiegen.
Gen Morgen war es, als ob Tiere brüllten
Doch ziemlich weit weg. Später kamen Stunden
Wo es ganz still war. Langsam fraß der Wald
In leichtem Wind, bei guter Sonne, still
Die Wiesen in den nächsten Wochen auf.

VOM ARMEN B.B.

1
Ich, Bertolt Brecht, bin aus den schwarzen Wäldern.
Meine Mutter trug mich in die Städte hinein
Als ich in ihrem Leibe lag. Und die Kälte der Wälder
Wird in mir bis zu meinem Absterben sein.

2
In der Asphaltstadt bin ich daheim. Von allem Anfang
Versehen mit jedem Sterbsakrament:
Mit Zeitungen. Und Tabak. Und Branntwein.
Mißtrauisch und faul und zufrieden am End.

The branches grew and the horrible tangle
Slowly grew over them. Later, at evening
Which was darker because of the foliage growing
They sat silent with fear, like apes in
Their cages, dead beat with hunger.
The tangle of branches grew that night. But there was probably moonlight
For it was still quite light; they could still see each other.
Only towards morning the stuff was so dense that
They never saw each other again before they died.
The next day a singing rose from the forest
Muffled and waning. Probably they sang to each other.
That night it grew stiller. The oxen too were silent.
Towards morning it was as if beasts bellowed
But fairly far off. Later came hours
When all was quiet. The forest slowly
In the gentle wind and the good sun, quietly
Ate up the meadows in the weeks that came.

Translated by Frank Jellinek

OF POOR B.B.

1
I, Bertolt Brecht, came out of the black forests.
My mother moved me into the cities as I lay
Inside her body. And the coldness of the forests
Will be inside me till my dying day.

2
In the asphalt city I'm at home. From the very start
Provided with every last sacrament:
With newspapers. And tobacco. And brandy.
To the end mistrustful, lazy and content.

3
Ich bin zu den Leuten freundlich. Ich setze
Einen steifen Hut auf nach ihrem Brauch.
Ich sage: es sind ganz besonders riechende Tiere
Und ich sage: es macht nichts, ich bin es auch.

4
In meine leeren Schaukelstühle vormittags
Setze ich mir mitunter ein paar Frauen
Und ich betrachte sie sorglos und sage ihnen:
In mir habt ihr einen, auf den könnt ihr nicht bauen.

5
Gegen abends versammle ich um mich Männer
Wir reden uns da mit »Gentleman« an
Sie haben ihre Füße auf meinen Tischen
Und sagen: es wird besser mit uns. Und ich frage nicht: wann.

6
Gegen Morgen in der grauen Frühe pissen die Tannen
Und ihr Ungeziefer, die Vögel, fängt an zu schrein.
Um die Stunde trink ich mein Glas in der Stadt aus und schmeiße
Den Tabakstummel weg und schlafe beunruhigt ein.

7
Wir sind gesessen ein leichtes Geschlechte
In Häusern, die für unzerstörbare galten
(So haben wir gebaut die langen Gehäuse des Eilands Manhattan
Und die dünnen Antennen, die das Atlantische Meer unterhalten).

8
Von diesen Städten wird bleiben: der durch sie hindurchging,
   der Wind!
Fröhlich machet das Haus den Esser: er leert es.
Wir wissen, daß wir Vorläufige sind
Und nach uns wird kommen: nichts Nennenswertes.

3
I'm polite and friendly to people. I put on
A hard hat because that's what they do.
I say: they are animals with a quite peculiar smell
And I say: does it matter? I am too.

4
Before noon on my empty rocking chairs
I'll sit a woman or two, and with an untroubled eye
Look at them steadily and say to them:
Here you have someone on whom you can't rely.

5
Towards evening it's men that I gather round me
And then we address one another as "gentlemen."
They're resting their feet on my table tops
And say: things will get better for us. And I don't ask when.

6
In the gray light before morning the pine trees piss
And their vermin, the birds, raise their twitter and cheep.
At that hour in the city I drain my glass, then throw
The cigar butt away and worriedly go to sleep.

7
We have sat, an easy generation
In houses held to be indestructible
(Thus we built those tall boxes on the island of Manhattan
And those thin aerials that amuse the Atlantic swell).

8
Of those cities will remain what passed through them,
    the wind!
The house makes glad the eater: he clears it out.
We know that we're only tenants, provisional ones
And after us there will come: nothing worth talking about.

9
Bei den Erdbeben, die kommen werden, werde ich hoffentlich
Meine Virginia nicht ausgehen lassen durch Bitterkeit
Ich, Bertolt Brecht, in die Asphaltstädte verschlagen
Aus den schwarzen Wäldern in meiner Mutter in früher Zeit.

9
In the earthquakes to come, I very much hope
I shall keep my cigar alight, embittered or no
I, Bertolt Brecht, carried off to the asphalt cities
From the black forests inside my mother long ago.

Translated by Michael Hamburger

From *Poems* Written between 1913 and 1926

DER NACHGEBORENE

Ich gestehe es: ich
Habe keine Hoffnung.
Die Blinden reden von einem Ausweg. Ich
Sehe.
Wenn die Irrtümer verbraucht sind
Sitzt als letzter Gesellschafter
Uns das Nichts gegenüber.

DER 4. PSALM

1. Was erwartet man noch von mir?
Ich habe alle Patiencen gelegt, alles Kirschwasser gespieen
Alle Bücher in den Ofen gestopft
Alle Weiber geliebt, bis sie wie der Leviathan gestunken haben.
Ich bin schon ein großer Heiliger, mein Ohr ist so faul, daß es nächstens einmal abbricht.
Warum ist also nicht Ruhe? Warum stehen immer noch die Leute im Hof wie Kehrrichttonnen—wartend, daß man etwas hineingibt?
Ich habe zu verstehen gegeben, daß man das Hohelied von mir nicht mehr erwarten darf.
Auf die Käufer habe ich die Polizei gehetzt.
Wer immer es ist, den ihr sucht: ich bin es nicht.

2. Ich bin der praktischste von allen meinen Brüdern—
Und mit m e i n e m Kopf fängt es an!
Meine Brüder waren grausam, ich bin der grausamste—
Und i c h weine nachts!

BORN LATER

I admit it: I
Have no hope.
The blind talk of a way out. I
See.

When the errors have been used up
As our last companion, facing us
Sits nothingness.

Translated by Michael Hamburger

THE FOURTH PSALM

1 What do people still expect of me?
I have played all the patiences, spat out all the kirsch
Stuffed all the books into the stove
Loved all the women till they stank like Leviathan.
Truly I am a great saint, my ear is so rotten it will
soon drop off.
So why is there no peace? Why do the people stand in the
yard like rubbish bins—waiting for something to be
put into them?
I have made it plain it is no use any more to expect the Song
of Songs from me.
I have set the police on the buyers.
Whoever it is you are looking for, it is not me.

2 I am the most practical of all my brothers—
And it all starts in *my* head!
My brothers were cruel, I am the cruellest
And it is *I* who weep at night!

3. Mit den Gesetzestafeln sind die Laster entzweigegangen.
Man schläft schon bei seiner Schwester ohne rechte Freude.
Der Mord ist vielen zu mühsam
Das Dichten ist zu allgemein.
Bei der Unsicherheit aller Verhältnisse
Ziehen es viele vor, die Wahrheit zu sagen
Aus Unkenntnis der Gefahr.
Die Kurtisanen pökeln Fleisch ein für den Winter
Und der Teufel holt seine besten Leute nicht mehr ab.

ENTDECKUNG AN EINER JUNGEN FRAU

Des Morgens nüchterner Abschied, eine Frau
Kühl zwischen Tür und Angel, kühl besehn.
Da sah ich: eine Strähn in ihrem Haar war grau
Ich konnt mich nicht entschließen mehr zu gehn.

Stumm nahm ich ihre Brust, und als sie fragte
Warum ich Nachtgast nach Verlauf der Nacht
Nicht gehen wolle, denn so war's gedacht
Sah ich sie unumwunden an und sagte:

Ist's nur noch eine Nacht, will ich noch bleiben
Doch nütze deine Zeit; das ist das Schlimme
Daß du so zwischen Tür und Angel stehst.

Und laß uns die Gespräche rascher treiben
Denn wir vergaßen ganz, daß du vergehst.
Und es verschlug Begierde mir die Stimme.

3 When the tables of the law broke, so did all vices.
Even sleeping with one's sister is no fun any more.
Murder is too much trouble for many
Writing poems is too common.
Since everything is too uncertain
Many prefer to tell the truth
Being ignorant of the danger.
The courtesans pickle meat for the winter
And the devil no longer carries away his best people.

Translated by Christopher Middleton

DISCOVERY ABOUT A YOUNG WOMAN

Next day's subdued farewell: she standing there
Cool on the threshold, coolly looked at too
When I observed a grey strand in her hair
And found I could not bring myself to go.

Silent I took her breast, and when she wondered
Why I, who'd been her guest that night in bed
Was not prepared to leave as we had said
I looked her straight between the eyes and answered:

It's only one more night that I'll be staying
But use your time; the fact is, you've provoked me
Standing poised on the threshold in that way.

And let us speed up what we've got to say
For both of us forgot that you're decaying.
With that my voice gave out, and longing choked me.

Translated by John Willett

From *Poems* Written between
1926 and 1933

VIER AUFFORDERUNGEN AN EINEN MANN VON VERSCHIEDENER SEITE ZU VERSCHIEDENEN ZEITEN

Hier hast du ein Heim
Hier ist Platz für deine Sachen
Stelle die Möbel um nach deinem Geschmack
Sage, was du brauchst
Da ist der Schlüssel
Hier bleibe.

Es ist eine Stube da für uns alle
Und für dich ein Zimmer mit einem Bett
Du kannst mitarbeiten im Hof
Du hast deinen eigenen Teller
Bleibe bei uns.

Hier ist deine Schlafstelle
Das Bett ist noch ganz frisch
Es lag erst ein Mann drin.
Wenn du heikel bist
Schwenke deinen Zinnlöffel in dem Bottich da
Dann ist er wie ein frischer
Bleibe ruhig bei uns.

Das ist die Kammer
Mach schnell, oder du kannst auch dableiben
Eine Nacht, aber das kostet extra.
Ich werde dich nicht stören
Übrigens bin ich nicht krank.
Du bist hier so gut aufgehoben wie woanders.
Du kannst also dableiben.

FOUR INVITATIONS TO A MAN AT DIFFERENT TIMES FROM DIFFERENT QUARTERS

There's a home for you here
There's a room for your things.
Move the furniture about to suit yourself
Tell us what you need
Here is the key
Stay here.

There's a parlour for us all
And for you a room with a bed
You can work with us in the yard
You have your own plate
Stay with us.

Here's where you're to sleep
The sheets are still clean
They've only been slept in once.
If you're fussy
Rinse your tin spoon in the bucket there
It'll be as good as new
You're welcome to stay with us.

That's the room
Hurry up, or you can also stay
The night, but that costs extra.
I shan't disturb you
By the way, I'm not ill.
You'll be as well off here as anywhere else
So you might as well stay.

Translated by Frank Jellinek

DAS FRÜHJAHR

1
Das Frühjahr kommt.
Das Spiel der Geschlechter erneuert sich
Die Liebenden finden sich zusammen.
Schon die sacht umfassende Hand des Geliebten
Macht die Brust des Mädchens erschauern.
Ihr flüchtiger Blick verführt ihn.

2
In neuem Lichte
Erscheint die Landschaft den Liebenden im Frühjahr.
In großer Höhe werden die ersten
Schwärme der Vögel gesichtet.
Die Luft ist schon warm.
Die Tage werden lang und die
Wiesen bleiben lang hell.

3
Maßlos ist das Wachstum der Bäume und Gräser
Im Frühjahr.
Ohne Unterlaß fruchtbar
Ist der Wald, sind die Wiesen, die Felder.
Und es gebiert die Erde das Neue
Ohne Vorsicht.

DIE NACHTLAGER

Ich höre, daß in New York
An der Ecke der 26. Straße und des Broadway
Während der Wintermonate jeden Abend ein Mann steht

THE SPRING

1
Springtime is coming.
The play of the sexes renews itself
That's when the lovers start to come together.
One gentle caress from the hand of her loved one
Has the girl's breast starting to tingle.
Her least glance will overwhelm him.

2
A new-found light
Reveals the countryside to lovers in springtime.
At a great height the first
Flocks of birds are sighted.
The air's turning warm.
The days are getting long and the
Fields stay light a long time.

3
Boundless is the growth of all trees and all grasses
In springtime.
Incessantly fruitful
Is the land, are the meadows, the forest.
And the earth gives birth to the new
Heedless of caution.

Translated by John Willett

A BED FOR THE NIGHT

I hear that in New York
At the corner of 26th Street and Broadway
A man stands every evening during the winter months

Und den Obdachlosen, die sich ansammeln
Durch Bitten an Vorübergehende ein Nachtlager verschafft.

Die Welt wird dadurch nicht anders
Die Beziehungen zwischen den Menschen bessern sich nicht
Das Zeitalter der Ausbeutung wird dadurch nicht verkürzt
Aber einige Männer haben ein Nachtlager
Der Wind wird von ihnen eine Nacht lang abgehalten
Der ihnen zugedachte Schnee fällt auf die Straße.

Leg das Buch nicht nieder, der du das liesest, Mensch.

Einige Menschen haben ein Nachtlager
Der Wind wird von ihnen eine Nacht lang abgehalten
Der ihnen zugedachte Schnee fällt auf die Straße
Aber die Welt wird dadurch nicht anders
Die Beziehungen zwischen den Menschen bessern sich dadurch nicht
Das Zeitalter der Ausbeutung wird dadurch nicht verkürzt.

VON ALLEN WERKEN

Von allen Werken die liebsten
Sind mir die gebrauchten.
Die Kupfergefäße mit den Beulen und den abgeplatteten Rändern
Die Messer und Gabeln, deren Holzgriffe
Abgegriffen sind von vielen Händen: solche Formen
Schienen mir die edelsten. So auch die Steinfliesen um alte Häuser
Welche niedergetreten sind von vielen Füßen, abgeschliffen
Und zwischen denen Grasbüschel wachsen, das
Sind glückliche Werke.

Eingegangen in den Gebrauch der vielen
Oftmals verändert, verbessern sie ihre Gestalt und werden köstlich

And gets beds for the homeless there
By appealing to passers-by.

It won't change the world
It won't improve relations among men
It will not shorten the age of exploitation
But a few men have a bed for the night
For a night the wind is kept from them
The snow meant for them falls on the roadway.

Don't put down the book on reading this, man.

A few people have a bed for the night
For a night the wind is kept from them
The snow meant for them falls on the roadway
But it won't change the world
It won't improve relations among men
It will not shorten the age of exploitation.

Translated by Georg Rapp

OF ALL THE WORKS OF MAN

Of all the works of man I like best
Those which have been used.
The copper pots with their dents and flattened edges
The knives and forks whose wooden handles
Have been worn away by many hands: such forms
Seemed to me the noblest. So too the flagstones round old houses
Trodden by many feet, ground down
And with tufts of grass growing between them: these
Are happy works.

Absorbed into the service of the many
Frequently altered, they improve their shape, grow precious

Weil oftmals gekostet.
Selbst die Bruchstücke von Plastiken
Mit ihren abgehauenen Händen liebe ich. Auch sie
Lebten mir. Wenn auch fallen gelassen, wurden sie doch getragen.
Wenn auch überrannt, standen sie doch nicht zu hoch.
Die halbzerfallenen Bauwerke
Haben wieder das Aussehen von noch nicht vollendeten
Groß geplanten: ihre schönen Maße
Sind schon zu ahnen; sie bedürfen aber
Noch unseres Verständnisses. Andrerseits
Haben sie schon gedient, ja, sind schon überwunden.
  Dies alles
Beglückt mich.

Because so often appreciated.
Even broken pieces of sculpture
With their hands lopped off, are dear to me. They too
Were alive for me. They were dropped, yet they were also carried.
They were knocked down, yet they never stood too high.

Half ruined buildings once again take on
The look of buildings waiting to be finished
Generously planned: their fine proportions
Can already be guessed at, but they still
Need our understanding. At the same time
They have already served, indeed have already been overcome.
   All this
Delights me.

Team Translation

From *Poems* Written between 1933 and 1938

AUSSCHLIEßLICH WEGEN DER ZUNEHMENDEN UNORDNUNG

Ausschließlich wegen der zunehmenden Unordnung
In unseren Städten des Klassenkampfs
Haben etliche von uns in diesen Jahren beschlossen
Nicht mehr zu reden von Hafenstädten, Schnee auf den
  Dächern, Frauen
Geruch reifer Äpfel im Keller, Empfindungen des Fleisches
All dem, was den Menschen rund macht und menschlich
Sondern zu reden nur mehr von der Unordnung
Also einseitig zu werden, dürr, verstrickt in die Geschäfte
Der Politik und das trockene »unwürdige« Vokabular
Der dialektischen Ökonomie
Damit nicht dieses furchtbare gedrängte Zusammensein
Von Schneefällen (sie sind nicht nur kalt, wir wissen's)
Ausbeutung, verlocktem Fleisch und Klassenjustiz eine Billigung
So vielseitiger Welt in uns erzeuge, Lust an
Den Widersprüchen solch blutigen Lebens
Ihr versteht.

ÜBER DIE GEWALT

Der reißende Strom wird gewalttätig genannt
Aber das Flußbett, das ihn einengt
Nennt keiner gewalttätig.

Der Sturm, der die Birken biegt
Gilt für gewalttätig
Aber wie ist es mit dem Sturm
Der die Rücken der Straßenarbeiter biegt?

SOLELY BECAUSE OF THE INCREASING DISORDER

Solely because of the increasing disorder
In our cities of class struggle
Some of us have now decided
To speak no more of cities by the sea, snow on roofs, women
The smell of ripe apples in cellars, the senses of the flesh, all
That makes a man round and human
But to speak in future only about the disorder
And so become one-sided, reduced, enmeshed in the business
Of politics and the dry, »indecorous« vocabulary
Of dialectical economics
So that this awful cramped coexistence
Of snowfalls (they're not merely cold, we know)
Exploitation, the lured flesh, class justice, should not engender
Approval of a world so many-sided; delight in
The contradictions of so bloodstained a life
You understand.

Translated by Frank Jellinek

ON VIOLENCE

The headlong stream is termed violent
But the river bed hemming it in is
Termed violent by no one.

The storm that bends the birch trees
Is held to be violent
But how about the storm
That bends the backs of the roadworkers?

Translated by John Willett

From *Svendborg Poems* (1939)

AUF DER MAUER STAND MIT KREIDE

Sie wollen den Krieg.
Der es geschrieben hat
Ist schon gefallen.

GENERAL, DEIN TANK IST EIN STARKER WAGEN

Er bricht einen Wald nieder und zermalmt hundert Menschen.
Aber er hat einen Fehler:
Er braucht einen Fahrer.

General, dein Bombenflugzeug ist stark.
Es fliegt schneller als ein Sturm und trägt mehr als ein Elefant.
Aber es hat einen Fehler:
Es braucht einen Monteur.

General, der Mensch ist sehr brauchbar.
Er kann fliegen und er kann töten.
Aber er hat einen Fehler:
Er kann denken.

LIED DER STARENSCHWÄRME

1
Wir sind aufgebrochen im Monat Oktober
In der Provinz Suiyuan
Wir sind rasch geflogen in südlicher Richtung, ohne abzuweichen
Durch vier Provinzen fünf Tage lang.
Fliegt rascher, die Ebenen warten

ON THE WALL WAS CHALKED

They want war.
The man who wrote it
Has already fallen.

Team Translation

GENERAL, YOUR TANK IS A POWERFUL VEHICLE

It smashes down forests and crushes a hundred men.
But it has one defect:
It needs a driver.

General, your bomber is powerful.
It flies faster than a storm and carries more than an elephant.
But it has one defect:
It needs a mechanic.

General, man is very useful.
He can fly and he can kill.
But he has one defect:
He can think.

Translated by Lee Baxandall

SONG OF THE FLOCKS OF STARLINGS

1
We set out in the month of October
In the province of Suiyan
We flew fast in a southerly direction straight
Through four provinces, taking five days.
   Fly faster, the plains are waiting

Die Kälte nimmt zu und
Dort ist Wärme.

2
Wir sind aufgebrochen und waren achttausend
Aus der Provinz Suiyuan
Wir sind mehr geworden täglich um Tausende, je weiter wir kamen
Durch vier Provinzen fünf Tage lang.
Fliegt rascher, die Ebenen warten
Die Kälte nimmt zu und
Dort ist Wärme.

3
Wir überfliegen jetzt die Ebene
In der Provinz Hunan
Wir sehen unter uns große Netze und wissen
Wohin wir geflogen sind fünf Tage lang:
Die Ebenen haben gewartet
Die Wärme nimmt zu und
Der Tod ist uns sicher.

DER PFLAUMENBAUM

Im Hofe steht ein Pflaumenbaum
Der ist klein, man glaubt es kaum.
Er hat ein Gitter drum
So tritt ihn keiner um.

Der Kleine kann nicht größer wer'n.
Ja größer wer'n, das möcht er gern.
's ist keine Red davon
Er hat zu wenig Sonn.

The cold increases and
There it is warm.

2
We set out, eight thousand of us
From the province of Suiyan
We grew by thousands each day, the farther we came
Through four provinces, taking five days.
  Fly faster, the plains are waiting
  The cold increases and
  There it is warm.

3
Now we are flying over the plain
In the province of Hunan
We see great nets beneath us and know
Where we have flown to, taking five days:
  The plains have waited
  The warmth increases and
  Our death is certain.

Translated by Michael Hamburger

THE PLUM TREE

The plum tree in the yard's so small
It's hardly like a tree at all.
Yet there it is, railed round
To keep it safe and sound.

The poor thing can't grow any more
Though if it could it would for sure.
There's nothing to be done
It gets too little sun.

Den Pflaumenbaum glaubt man ihm kaum
Weil er nie eine Pflaume hat
Doch er ist ein Pflaumenbaum
Man kennt es an dem Blatt.

FRAGEN EINES LESENDEN ARBEITERS

Wer baute das siebentorige Theben?
In den Büchern stehen die Namen von Königen.
Haben die Könige die Felsbrocken herbeigeschleppt?
Und das mehrmals zerstörte Babylon
Wer baute es so viele Male auf? In welchen Häusern
Des goldstrahlenden Lima wohnten die Bauleute?
Wohin gingen an dem Abend, wo die chinesische Mauer fertig war
Die Maurer? Das große Rom
Ist voll von Triumphbögen. Wer errichtete sie? Über wen
Triumphierten die Cäsaren? Hatte das vielbesungene Byzanz
Nur Paläste für seine Bewohner? Selbst in dem sagenhaften Atlantis
Brüllten in der Nacht, wo das Meer es verschlang
Die Ersaufenden nach ihren Sklaven.

Der junge Alexander eroberte Indien.
Er allein?
Cäsar schlug die Gallier.
Hatte er nicht wenigstens einen Koch bei sich?
Philipp von Spanien weinte, als seine Flotte
Untergegangen war. Weinte sonst niemand?
Friedrich der Zweite siegte im Siebenjährigen Krieg. Wer
Siegte außer ihm?

Jede Seite ein Sieg.
Wer kochte den Siegesschmaus?
Alle zehn Jahre ein großer Mann.
Wer bezahlte die Spesen?

The plum tree never bears a plum
So it's not easy to believe.
It is a plum tree all the same
One tells it by the leaf.

Team Translation

QUESTIONS FROM A WORKER WHO READS

Who built Thebes of the seven gates?
In the books you will find the names of kings.
Did the kings haul up the lumps of rock?
And Babylon, many times demolished
Who raised it up so many times? In what houses
Of gold-glittering Lima did the builders live?
Where, the evening that the Wall of China was finished
Did the masons go? Great Rome
Is full of triumphal arches. Who erected them? Over whom
Did the Caesars triumph? Had Byzantium, much praised in song
Only palaces for its inhabitants? Even in fabled Atlantis
The night the ocean engulfed it
The drowning still bawled for their slaves.

The young Alexander conquered India.
Was he alone?
Caesar beat the Gauls.
Did he not have even a cook with him?
Philip of Spain wept when his armada
Went down. Was he the only one to weep?
Frederick the Second won the Seven Years' War. Who
Else won it?

Every page a victory.
Who cooked the feast for the victors?
Every ten years a great man.
Who paid the bill?

So viele Berichte
So viele Fragen.

LEGENDE VON DER ENTSTEHUNG DES BUCHES TAOTEKING AUF DEM WEG DES LAOTSE IN DIE EMIGRATION

1
Als er siebzig war und war gebrechlich
Drängte es den Lehrer doch nach Ruh
Denn die Güte war im Lande wieder einmal schwächlich
Und die Bosheit nahm an Kräften wieder einmal zu.
Und er gürtete den Schuh.

2
Und er packte ein, was er so brauchte:
Wenig. Doch es wurde dies und das.
So die Pfeife, die er immer abends rauchte
Und das Büchlein, das er immer las.
Weißbrot nach dem Augenmaß.

3
Freute sich des Tals noch einmal und vergaß es
Als er ins Gebirg den Weg einschlug.
Und sein Ochse freute sich des frischen Grases
Kauend, während er den Alten trug.
Denn dem ging es schnell genug.

4
Doch am vierten Tag im Felsgesteine
Hat ein Zöllner ihm den Weg verwehrt:
»Kostbarkeiten zu verzollen?« – »Keine.«
Und der Knabe, der den Ochsen führte, sprach: »Er hat gelehrt.«
Und so war auch das erklärt.

So many reports.
So many questions.

Translated by Michael Hamburger

LEGEND OF THE ORIGIN OF THE BOOK TAO-TE-CHING ON
LAO-TSU'S ROAD INTO EXILE

1
Once he was seventy and getting brittle
Quiet retirement seemed the teacher's due.
In his country goodness had been weakening a little
And the wickedness was gaining ground anew.
So he buckled on his shoe.

2
And he packed up what he would be needing:
Not much. But enough to travel light.
Items like the book that he was always reading
And the pipe he used to smoke at night.
Bread as much as he thought right.

3
Gladly looked back at his valley, then forgot it
As he turned to take the mountain track.
And the ox was glad of the fresh grass it spotted
Munching, with the old man on its back
Happy that the pace was slack.

4
Four days out among the rocks, a barrier
Where a customs man made them report.
"What valuables have you to declare here?"
And the boy leading the ox explained: "The old man taught".
Nothing at all, in short.

5
Doch der Mann in einer heitren Regung
Fragte noch: »Hat er was rausgekriegt?«
Sprach der Knabe: »Daß das weiche Wasser in Bewegung
Mit der Zeit den mächtigen Stein besiegt.
Du verstehst, das Harte unterliegt.«

6
Daß er nicht das letzte Tageslicht verlöre
Trieb der Knabe nun den Ochsen an.
Und die drei verschwanden schon um eine schwarze Föhre
Da kam plötzlich Fahrt in unsern Mann
Und er schrie: »He, du! Halt an!

7
Was ist das mit diesem Wasser, Alter?«
Hielt der Alte: »Intressiert es dich?«
Sprach der Mann: »Ich bin nur Zollverwalter
Doch wer wen besiegt, das intressiert auch mich.
Wenn du's weißt, dann sprich!

8
Schreib mir's auf! Diktier es diesem Kinde!
So was nimmt man doch nicht mit sich fort.
Da gibt's doch Papier bei uns und Tinte
Und ein Nachtmahl gibt es auch: ich wohne dort.
Nun, ist das ein Wort?«

9
Über seine Schulter sah der Alte
Auf den Mann: Flickjoppe. Keine Schuh.
Und die Stirne eine einzige Falte.
Ach, kein Sieger trat da auf ihn zu.
Und er murmelte: »Auch du?«

5
Then the man, in cheerful disposition
Asked again: "How did he make out, pray?"
Said the boy: "He learnt how quite soft water, by attrition
Over the years will grind strong rocks away.
In other words, that hardness must lose the day."

6
Then the boy tugged at the ox to get it started
Anxious to move on, for it was late.
But as they disappeared behind a fir tree which they skirted
Something suddenly began to agitate
The man, who shouted: "Hey, you! Wait!"

7
"What was that you said about the water?"
Old man pauses: "Do you want to know?"
Man replies: "I'm not at all important
Who wins or loses interests me, though.
If you've found out, say so.

8
"Write it down. Dictate it to your boy there.
Once you've gone, who can we find out from?
There are pen and ink for your employ here
And a supper we can share; this is my home.
It's a bargain: come!"

9
Turning round, the old man looks in sorrow
At the man. Worn tunic. Got no shoes.
And his forehead just a single furrow.
Ah, no winner this he's talking to.
And he softly says: "You too?"

10
Eine höfliche Bitte abzuschlagen
War der Alte, wie es schien, zu alt.
Denn er sagte laut: »Die etwas fragen
Die verdienen Antwort.« Sprach der Knabe: »Es wird auch
 schon kalt.«
»Gut, ein kleiner Aufenthalt.«

11
Und von seinem Ochsen stieg der Weise
Sieben Tage schrieben sie zu zweit.
Und der Zöllner brachte Essen (und er fluchte nur
 noch leise
Mit den Schmugglern in der ganzen Zeit).
Und dann war's soweit.

12
Und dem Zöllner händigte der Knabe
Eines Morgens einundachtzig Sprüche ein
Und mit Dank für eine kleine Reisegabe
Bogen sie um jene Föhre ins Gestein.
Sagt jetzt: kann man höflicher sein?

13
Aber rühmen wir nicht nur den Weisen
Dessen Name auf dem Buche prangt!
Denn man muß dem Weisen seine Weisheit erst entreißen.
Darum sei der Zöllner auch bedankt:
Er hat sie ihm abverlangt.

10
Snubbing of politely put suggestions
Seems to be unheard of by the old.
For the old man said: "Those who ask questions
Deserve answers." Then the boy: "What's more, it's turning cold."
"Right. Then get my bed unrolled."

11
Stiffly from his ox the sage dismounted.
Seven days he wrote there with his friend.
And the man brought them their meals (and all the smugglers were astounded
At what seemed this sudden lenient trend).
And then came the end.

12
And the boy handed over what they'd written—
Eighty-one sayings—early one day.
And they thanked the man for the alms he'd given
Went round that fir and climbed the rocky way.
Who was so polite as they?

13
But the honour should not be restricted
To the sage whose name is clearly writ.
For a wise man's wisdom needs to be extracted.
So the customs man deserves his bit.
It was he who called for it.

Translated by John Willett

AN DIE NACHGEBORENEN

1
Wirklich, ich lebe in finsteren Zeiten!
Das arglose Wort ist töricht. Eine glatte Stirn
Deutet auf Unempfindlichkeit hin. Der Lachende
Hat die furchtbare Nachricht
Nur noch nicht empfangen.

Was sind das für Zeiten, wo
Ein Gespräch über Bäume fast ein Verbrechen ist
Weil es ein Schweigen über so viele Untaten einschließt!
Der dort ruhig über die Straße geht
Ist wohl nicht mehr erreichbar für seine Freunde
Die in Not sind?

Es ist wahr: ich verdiene noch meinen Unterhalt
Aber glaubt mir: das ist nur ein Zufall. Nichts
Von dem, was ich tue, berechtigt mich dazu, mich satt zu essen.
Zufällig bin ich verschont. (Wenn mein Glück aussetzt
Bin ich verloren.)

Man sagt mir: iß und trink du! Sei froh, daß du hast!
Aber wie kann ich essen und trinken, wenn
Ich es dem Hungernden entreiße, was ich esse, und
Mein Glas Wasser einem Verdurstenden fehlt?
Und doch esse und trinke ich.

Ich wäre gerne auch weise
In den alten Büchern steht, was weise ist:
Sich aus dem Streit der Welt halten und die kurze Zeit
Ohne Furcht verbringen
Auch ohne Gewalt auskommen
Böses mit Gutem vergelten

TO THOSE BORN LATER

1
Truly, I live in dark times!
The guileless word is folly. A smooth forehead
Suggests insensitivity. The man who laughs
Has simply not yet had
The terrible news.

What kind of times are they, when
A talk about trees is almost a crime
Because it implies silence about so many horrors?
That man there calmly crossing the street
Is already perhaps beyond the reach of his friends
Who are in need?

It is true I still earn my keep
But, believe me, that is only an accident. Nothing
I do gives me the right to eat my fill.
By chance I've been spared. (If my luck breaks, I am lost.)

They say to me: Eat and drink! Be glad you have it!
But how can I eat and drink if I snatch what I eat
From the starving, and
My glass of water belongs to one dying of thirst?
And yet I eat and drink.

I would also like to be wise.
In the old books it says what wisdom is:
To shun the strife of the world and to live out
Your brief time without fear
Also to get along without violence
To return good for evil
Not to fulfill your desires but to forget them

Seine Wünsche nicht erfüllen, sondern vergessen
Gilt für weise.
Alles das kann ich nicht:
Wirklich, ich lebe in finsteren Zeiten!

2
In die Städte kam ich zu der Zeit der Unordnung
Als da Hunger herrschte.
Unter die Menschen kam ich zu der Zeit des Aufruhrs
Und ich empörte mich mit ihnen.
So verging meine Zeit
Die auf Erden mir gegeben war.

Mein Essen aß ich zwischen den Schlachten
Schlafen legte ich mich unter die Mörder
Der Liebe pflegte ich achtlos
Und die Natur sah ich ohne Geduld.
So verging meine Zeit
Die auf Erden mir gegeben war.

Die Straßen führten in den Sumpf zu meiner Zeit
Die Sprache verriet mich dem Schlächter
Ich vermochte nur wenig. Aber die Herrschenden
Saßen ohne mich sicherer, das hoffte ich.
So verging meine Zeit
Die auf Erden mir gegeben war.

Die Kräfte waren gering. Das Ziel
Lag in großer Ferne
Es war deutlich sichtbar, wenn auch für mich
Kaum zu erreichen.
So verging meine Zeit
Die auf Erden mir gegeben war.

Is accounted wise.
All this I cannot do:
Truly, I live in dark times.

2
I came to the cities in a time of disorder
When hunger reigned there.
I came among men in a time of revolt
And I rebelled with them.
So passed my time
Which had been given to me on earth.

My food I ate between battles
To sleep I lay down among murderers
Love I practised carelessly
And nature I looked at without patience.
So passed my time
Which had been given to me on earth.

All roads led into the mire in my time.
My tongue betrayed me to the butchers.
There was little I could do. But those in power
Sat safer without me: that was my hope.
So passed my time
Which had been given to me on earth.

Our forces were slight. Our goal
Lay far in the distance
It was clearly visible, though I myself
Was unlikely to reach it.
So passed my time
Which had been given to me on earth.

3
Ihr, die ihr auftauchen werdet aus der Flut
In der wir untergegangen sind
Gedenkt
Wenn ihr von unsern Schwächen sprecht
Auch der finsteren Zeit
Der ihr entronnen seid.

Gingen wir doch, öfter als die Schuhe die Länder wechselnd
Durch die Kriege der Klassen, verzweifelt
Wenn da nur Unrecht war und keine Empörung.

Dabei wissen wir ja:
Auch der Haß gegen die Niedrigkeit
Verzerrt die Züge.
Auch der Zorn über das Unrecht
Macht die Stimme heiser. Ach, wir
Die wir den Boden bereiten wollten für Freundlichkeit
Konnten selber nicht freundlich sein.

Ihr aber, wenn es soweit sein wird
Daß der Mensch dem Menschen ein Helfer ist
Gedenkt unsrer
Mit Nachsicht.

3
You who will emerge from the flood
In which we have gone under
Remember
When you speak of our failings
The dark time too
Which you have escaped.

For we went, changing countries oftener than our shoes
Through the wars of the classes, despairing
When there was injustice only, and no rebellion.

And yet we know:
Hatred, even of meanness
Contorts the features.
Anger, even against injustice
Makes the voice hoarse. Oh, we
Who wanted to prepare the ground for friendliness
Could not ourselves be friendly.

But you, when the time comes at last
And man is a helper to man
Thinks of us
With forebearance.

Team Translation

Interlude

Poems (Songs) from and about Plays

DAS LIED VON DER MOLDAU

Am Grunde der Moldau wandern die Steine
Es liegen drei Kaiser begraben in Prag.
Das Große bleibt groß nicht und klein nicht das Kleine.
Die Nacht hat zwölf Stunden, dann kommt schon der Tag.

Es wechseln die Zeiten. Die riesigen Pläne
Der Mächtigen kommen am Ende zum Halt.
Und gehn sie einher auch wie blutige Hähne
Es wechseln die Zeiten, da hilft kein Gewalt.

Am Grunde der Moldau wandern die Steine
Es liegen drei Kaiser begraben in Prag.
Das Große bleibt groß nicht und klein nicht das Kleine.
Die Nacht hat zwölf Stunden, dann kommt schon der Tag.

LIED VOM ACHTEN ELEFANTEN

Sieben Elefanten hatte Herr Dschin
Und da war dann noch der achte.
Sieben waren wild und der achte war zahm
Und der achte war's, der sie bewachte.
   Trabt schneller!
   Herr Dschin hat einen Wald
   Der muß vor Nacht gerodet sein
   Und Nacht ist jetzt schon bald!

Sieben Elefanten roden den Wald
Und Herr Dschin ritt hoch auf dem achten.
All den Tag Nummer acht stand faul auf der Wacht
Und sah zu, was sie hinter sich brachten.

THE SONG OF THE MOLDAU

The stones on the Moldau's bottom go shifting
In Prague three emperors molder away.
The top won't stay top, for the bottom is lifting
The night has twelve hours and is followed by day.

The times will be changing. The intricate plotting
Of people in power must finally fail.
Like bloodthirsty cocks though today they are strutting
The times will be changing, force cannot prevail.

The stones on the Moldau's bottom go shifting
In Prague three emperors molder away.
The top won't stay top, for the bottom is lifting
The night has twelve hours and is followed by day.

Translated by Max Knight and Joseph Fabry

SONG OF THE EIGHTH ELEPHANT

Elephants seven had Mr. Chin
Plus an eighth, an early riser.
Seven were wild and the eighth was tame
Number eight was the supervisor.
   Step lively!
   This wood is Mr. Chin's.
   You've got to clear it, root and branch
   Before the night begins.

Elephants seven cleared the wood
And on top of the eighth rode the master.
Lazy number eight spied from early to late
To make sure that the others worked faster.

Grabt schneller!
Herr Dschin hat einen Wald
Der muß vor Nacht gerodet sein
Und Nacht ist jetzt schon bald!

Sieben Elefanten wollten nicht mehr
Hatten satt das Bäumeabschlachten.
Herr Dschin war nervös, auf die sieben war er bös
Und gab ein Schaff Reis dem achten.
Was soll das?
Herr Dschin hat einen Wald
Der muß vor Nacht gerodet sein
Und Nacht ist jetzt schon bald!

Sieben Elefanten hatten keinen Zahn
Seinen Zahn hatte nur noch der achte.
Und Nummer acht war vorhanden, schlug die sieben zuschanden
Und Herr Dschin stand dahinten und lachte.
Grabt weiter!
Herr Dschin hat einen Wald
Der muß vor Nacht gerodet sein
Und Nacht ist jetzt schon bald!

DAS LIED VOM SANKT NIMMERLEINSTAG

Eines Tags, und das hat wohl ein jeder gehört
Der in ärmlicher Wiege lag
Kommt des armen Weibs Sohn auf 'nen goldenen Thron
Und der Tag heißt Sankt Nimmerleinstag.
Am Sankt Nimmerleinstag
Sitzt er auf 'nem goldenen Thron.

Dig harder!
This wood is Mr. Chin's.
You've got to clear it, root and branch
Before the night begins.

Elephants seven were thoroughly sick
Of uprooting little and big trees.
Old Chin in his heaven frowned down on the seven
To the eighth he fed barrels of chick peas.
   How come, sir?
   This wood is Mr. Chin's.
   You've got to clear it, root and branch
   Before the night begins.

Elephants seven had all lost their tusks.
Number eight had two tusks strong and flashing.
The eighth he rushed toward them and ruthlessly gored them
While the master sat up there laughing.
   Keep digging!
   This wood is Mr. Chin's.
   You've got to clear it, root and branch
   Before the night begins.

Translated by Ralph Manheim

THE SONG OF SAINT NEVERKIN'S DAY

There's a song that they tell of among the poor folk
Of this world that's so grim and gray
When the poor woman's son will ascend the king's throne
And that day is Saint Neverkin's Day.
   On Saint Neverkin's Day
   He'll sit on the king's golden throne.

Und an diesem Tag zahlt die Güte sich aus
Und die Schlechtigkeit kostet den Hals
Und Verdienst und Verdienen, die machen gute Mienen
Und tauschen Brot und Salz.
Am Sankt Nimmerleinstag
Da tauschen sie Brot und Salz.

Und das Gras sieht auf den Himmel hinab
Und den Fluß hinauf rollt der Kies
Und der Mensch ist nur gut. Ohne daß er mehr tut
Wird die Erde zum Paradies.
Am Sankt Nimmerleinstag
Wird die Erde zum Paradies.

Und an diesem Tag werd ich Flieger sein
Und ein General bist du.
Und du Mann mit zuviel Zeit kriegst endlich Arbeit
Und du armes Weib kriegst Ruh.
Am Sankt Nimmerleinstag
Kriegst armes Weib du Ruh.

Und weil wir gar nicht mehr warten können
Heißt es, alles dies sei
Nicht erst auf die Nacht um halb acht oder acht
Sondern schon beim Hahnenschrei.
Am Sankt Nimmerleinstag
Beim ersten Hahnenschrei.

LIED DES STÜCKSCHREIBERS

Ich bin ein Stückschreiber. Ich zeige
Was ich gesehen habe. Auf den Menschenmärkten
Habe ich gesehen, wie der Mensch gehandelt wird. Das
Zeige ich, ich, der Stückschreiber.

And on that famous day a man's goodness will pay
And his wickedness cost him his life.
Then desert and reward will sit down at one board
As cozy as husband and wife.
    On Saint Neverkin's Day
    As congenial as husband and wife.

And the grass will look down on the singing blue sky
And the pebbles will wander upstream.
Every man will be good, without work there'll be food
Life on earth will become a sweet dream.
    On Saint Neverkin's Day
    Life on earth will become a sweet dream.

On Saint Neverkin's Day I shall fly my own plane
And you will sit down with the best
And my unemployed friends will find jobs without end
And you, poor old woman, will rest.
    On Saint Neverkin's Day
    Poor woman, you will rest.

And because we can't wait one minute more
All this will come into sight
Not when the day has half passed away
But long before morning light.
    On Saint Neverkin's Day
    Long before morning light.

Translated by Ralph Manheim

THE PLAYWRIGHT'S SONG

I am a playwright. I show
What I have seen. In the man markets
I have seen how men are traded. That
I show, I, the playwright.

Wie sie zueinander ins Zimmer treten mit Plänen
Oder mit Gummiknüppeln oder mit Geld
Wie sie auf den Straßen stehen und warten
Wie sie einander Fallen bereiten
Voller Hoffnung
Wie sie Verabredungen treffen
Wie sie einander aufhängen
Wie sie sich lieben
Wie sie die Beute verteidigen
Wie sie essen
Das zeige ich.

Die Worte, die sie einander zurufen, berichte ich.
Was die Mutter dem Sohn sagt
Was der Unternehmer dem Unternommenen befiehlt
Was die Frau dem Mann antwortet
Alle die bittenden Worte, alle die herrischen
Die flehenden, die mißverständlichen
Die lügnerischen, die unwissenden
Die schönen, die verletzenden
Alle berichte ich.

Ich sehe da auftreten Schneefälle
Ich sehe da nach vorn kommen Erdbeben
Ich sehe da Berge stehen mitten im Wege
Und Flüsse sehe ich über die Ufer treten.
Aber die Schneefälle haben Hüte auf
Die Erdbeben haben Geld in der Brusttasche
Die Berge sind aus Fahrzeugen gestiegen
Und die reißenden Flüsse gebieten über Polizisten.
Das enthülle ich.

Um zeigen zu können, was ich sehe
Lese ich nach die Darstellungen anderer Völker und
    anderer Zeitalter.
Ein paar Stücke habe ich nachgeschrieben, genau

How they step into each other's rooms with schemes
Or rubber truncheons, or with cash
How they stand in the streets and wait
How they lay traps for one another
Full of hope
How they make appointments
How they hang each other
How they make love
How they defend their loot
How they eat
I show all that.

The words which they call out to each other I report.
What the mother says to her son
What the employer tells the employee
What the wife tells to her husband
All the begging words, all the commanding
The grovelling, the misleading
The lying, the unknowing
The winning, the wounding . . .
I report them all.

I see snowstorms making their entrances
I see earthquakes coming forward
I see mountains blocking the road
And rivers I see breaking their banks.
But the snowstorms have hats on
The earthquakes have money in their wallet
The mountains came in a conveyance
And the headlog rivers control the police.
That I reveal.

To learn how to show what I see
I read up the representations of other peoples and
    other periods.
One or two plays I have adapted, precisely

Prüfend die jeweilige Technik und mir einprägend
Das, was mir zustatten kommt.
Ich studierte die Darstellungen der großen Feudalen
Durch die Engländer, reicher Figuren
Denen die Welt dazu dient, sich groß zu entfalten.
Ich studierte die moralisierenden Spanier
Die Inder, Meister der schönen Empfindungen
Und die Chinesen, welche die Familien darstellen
Und die bunten Schicksale in den Städten.

Und so schnell wechselte zu meiner Zeit
Das Aussehen der Häuser und Städte, daß ein Wegfahren für
    zwei Jahre
Und ein Rückkehren eine Reise in eine andere Stadt war
Und in riesiger Masse wandelten die Menschen ihr Aussehen
In wenigen Jahren. Ich sah
Arbeiter in das Tor der Fabrik treten, und das Tor war hoch
Aber als sie herauskamen, mußten sie sich bücken.
Da sagte ich zu mir:
Alles wandelt sich und ist nur für seine Zeit.

Also gab ich jedem Schauplatz sein Kennzeichen
Und brannte jedem Fabrikhof seine Jahreszahl ein und
    jedem Zimmer
Wie die Hirten dem Vieh seine Zahl einbrennen, daß es
    erkannt wird.

Und auch den Sätzen, die da gesprochen wurden
Gab ich ihr Kennzeichen, so daß sie wurden wie Aussprüche
Der Vergänglichen, die man aufzeichnet
Damit sie nicht vergessen werden.

Was da die Frau sagte im Arbeitskittel
Über die Flugblätter gebeugt, in diesen Jahren
Und wie die Börsenleute mit ihren Schreibern sprachen
Die Hüte im Genick, gestern

Checking the technique of those times and absorbing
Whatever is of use to me.
I studied the portrayal of the great feudal figures
By the English, of rich individuals
To whom the world existed for their fuller development.
I studied the moralising Spaniards
The Indians, masters of beautiful sensations
And the Chinese, who portray the family
And the many-coloured destinies found in cities.

And so swiftly did the appearance of cities and houses
Change in my time that to go away for two years
And come back was like a trip to another city
And people in vast numberes changed their appearance
Within a few years. I saw
Workers enter the factory gates, and the gateway was tall
But when they came out they had to bend.
Then I told myself:
Everything alters and is for its own time only.

And so I gave each setting its recognition mark
And branded the figures of the year on each factory yard and
    each room
Like drovers who brand figures on their cattle to identify them.
And the sentences too that were spoken there
I gave recognition marks to, so that they became like the sayings
Of impermanent men which are set down
So that they may not be forgotten.

What the woman in overalls said during those years
Bent over her leaflets
And the way the brokers used yesterday to speak to
    their clerks
Hats on the backs of their heads
I marked with the impermanence of
Their year of origin.

Das versah ich mit dem Zeichen der Vergänglichkeit
Ihrer Jahreszahl.

Alles aber übergab ich dem Staunen
Selbst das Vertrauteste.
Daß die Mutter dem Kinde die Brust reichte
Das berichtete ich wie etwas, das keiner mir glauben wird.
Daß der Pförtner vor dem Frierenden die Tür zuschlug
Wie etwas, das noch keiner gesehen hat.

But all this I yielded up to astonishment
Even the most familiar part of it.
That a mother gave her child the breast
I reported like something no one would believe.
That a porter slammed the door in a freezing man's face
Like somebody nobody had ever seen.

Translated by John Willett

From *Poems* Written between 1938 and 1941

SCHLECHTE ZEIT FÜR LYRIK

Ich weiß doch: nur der Glückliche
Ist beliebt. Seine Stimme
Hört man gern. Sein Gesicht ist schön.

Der verkrüppelte Baum im Hof
Zeigt auf den schlechten Boden, aber
Die Vorübergehenden schimpfen ihn einen Krüppel
Doch mit Recht.

Die grünen Boote und die lustigen Segel des Sundes
Sehe ich nicht. Von allem
Sehe ich nur der Fischer rissiges Garnnetz.
Warum rede ich nur davon
Daß die vierzigjährige Häuslerin gekrümmt geht?
Die Brüste der Mädchen
Sind warm wie ehedem.

In meinem Lied ein Reim
Käme mir fast vor wie Übermut.

In mir streiten sich
Die Begeisterung über den blühenden Apfelbaum
Und das Entsetzen über die Reden des Anstreichers.
Aber nur das zweite
Drängt mich zum Schreibtisch.

SONETT NR. 1

Und nun ist Krieg, und unser Weg wird schwerer.
Du, die mir beigesellt, den Weg zu teilen

BAD TIME FOR POETRY

Yes, I know: only the happy man
Is liked. His voice
Is good to hear. His face is handsome.

The crippled tree in the yard
Shows that the soil is poor, yet
The passers-by abuse it for being crippled
And rightly so.

The green boats and the dancing sails on the Sound
Go unseen. Of it all
I see only the torn nets of the fishermen.
Why do I only record
That a village woman aged forty walks with a stoop?
The girls' breasts
Are as warm as ever.

In my poetry a rhyme
Would seem to me almost insolent.

Inside me contend
Delight at the apple tree in blossom
And horror at the house-painter's speeches.
But only the second
Drives me to my desk.

Team Translation

SONNET NO. 1

And now it's war; our path is growing steeper.
You, my companion sent to share the journey

Den schmalen oder breiten, ebnen oder steilen
Belehrte beide wir und beide Lehrer

Und beide flüchtend und mit gleichem Ziele
Wisse, was ich weiß: Dieses Ziel ist nicht
Mehr als der Weg, so daß, wenn einer fiele
Und ihn der andre fallen ließe, nur erpicht

Ans Ziel zu kommen, dieses Ziel verschwände
Nie mehr erkenntlich, nirgends zu erfragen!
Er liefe keuchend und am Ende stände

Er schweißbedeckt in einem grauen Nichts.
Dies dir an diesem Meilenstein zu sagen
Beauftrag ich die Muse des Gedichts.

1940 VI

Mein junger Sohn fragt mich: Soll ich Mathematik lernen?
Wozu, möchte ich sagen. Daß zwei Stück Brot mehr ist als eines
Das wirst du auch so merken.
Mein junger Sohn fragt mich: Soll ich Französisch lernen?
Wozu, möchte ich sagen. Dieses Reich geht unter. Und
Reibe du nur mit der Hand den Bauch und stöhne
Und man wird dich schon verstehen.
Mein junger Sohn fragt mich: Soll ich Geschichte lernen?
Wozu, möchte ich sagen. Lerne du deinen Kopf in die Erde stecken
Da wirst du vielleicht übrigbleiben.

Ja, lerne Mathematik, sage ich
Lerne Französisch, lerne Geschichte!

On broad or narrow roads, on smooth or stony
A student each of us, and each a teacher

And each now fleeing for the selfsame end
Know what I know: This end cannot be counted
More than the journey, so that if one fainted
And if the other left him, all intent

To gain his end, why, it would surely vanish
Not to be seen again, or found by asking.
Breathless he'd run until he stood in panic

Sweating, in gray and neutral nothingness.
To tell you this, and mark the point we're passing
I put my message in poetic dress.

Translated by John Willett

1940 VI

My young son asks me: Should I learn mathematics?
What for, I'm inclined to say. That two bits of bread are more than one
You'll notice anyway.
My young son asks me: Should I learn French?
What for, I'm inclined to say. That empire is going under.
Just rub your hand across your belly and groan
And you'll be understood all right.
My young son asks me: Should I learn history?
What for, I'm inclined to say. Learn to stick your head in the ground
Then maybe you'll come through.

Yes, learn mathematics, I tell him
Learn French, learn history!

Translated by Sammy McLean

From *Poems* Written between 1941 and 1947

DIE LANDSCHAFT DES EXILS

Aber auch ich auf dem letzten Boot
Sah noch den Frohsinn des Frührots im Takelzeug
Und der Delphine graulichte Leiber, tauchend
Aus der Japanischen See.
Und die Pferdewäglein mit dem Goldbeschlag
Und die rosa Armschleier der Matronen
In den Gassen des gezeichneten Manila
Sah auch der Flüchtling mit Freude.
Die Öltürme und dürstenden Gärten von Los Angeles
Und die abendlichen Schluchten Kaliforniens und die
   Obstmärkte
Ließen auch den Boten des Unglücks
Nicht kalt.

NACHDENKEND ÜBER DIE HÖLLE

Nachdenkend, wie ich höre, über die Hölle
Fand mein Bruder Shelley, sie sei ein Ort
Gleichend ungefähr der Stadt London. Ich
Der ich nicht in London lebe, sondern in Los Angeles
Finde, nachdenkend über die Hölle, sie muß
Noch mehr Los Angeles gleichen.

Auch in der Hölle
Gibt es, ich zweifle nicht, diese üppigen Gärten
Mit den Blumen, so groß wie Bäume, freilich verwelkend
Ohne Aufschub, wenn nicht gewässert mit sehr teurem
   Wasser. Und Obstmärkte
Mit ganzen Haufen von Früchten, die allerdings
Weder riechen noch schmecken. Und endlose Züge von Autos
Leichter als ihr eigener Schatten, schneller als

LANDSCAPE OF EXILE

But even I, on the last boat
Saw the gaiety of the dawn in the rigging
And the grayish bodies of dolphins emerge
From the Japanese Sea.

The little horsecarts with gilt decorations
And the pink sleeves of the matrons
In the alleys of doomed Manila
The fugitive beheld with joy.

The old derricks and the thirsty gardens of Los Angeles
And the ravines of California at evening and the fruit market
Did not leave the messenger of misfortune
unmoved.

Translated by H. R. Hays

ON THINKING ABOUT HELL

On thinking about Hell, I gather
My brother Shelley found it was a place
Much like the city of London. I
Who live in Los Angeles and not in London
Find, on thinking about Hell, that it must be
Still more like Los Angeles.

In Hell too
There are, I've no doubt, these luxuriant gardens
With flowers as big as trees, which of course wither
Unhesitatingly if not nourished with very expensive water.
   And fruit markets
With great heaps of fruit, albeit having
Neither smell nor taste. And endless processions of cars
Lighter than their own shadows, faster than

Törichte Gedanken, schimmernde Fahrzeuge, in denen
Rosige Leute, von nirgendher kommend, nirgendhin fahren.
Und Häuser, für Glückliche gebaut, daher leerstehend
Auch wenn bewohnt.
Auch die Häuser in der Hölle sind nicht alle häßlich.
Aber die Sorge, auf die Straße geworfen zu werden
Verzehrt die Bewohner der Villen nicht weniger als
Die Bewohner der Baracken.

DER DEMOKRATISCHE RICHTER

In Los Angeles vor den Richter, der die Leute examiniert
Die sich bemühen, Bürger der Vereinigten Staaten zu werden
Kam auch ein italienischer Gastwirt. Nach ernsthafter
  Vorbereitung
Leider behindert durch seine Unkenntnis der neuen Sprache
Antwortete er im Examen auf die Frage:
Was bedeutet das 8. Amendment? zögernd:
1492. Da das Gesetz die Kenntnis der Landessprache dem
  Bewerber vorschreibt
Wurde er abgewiesen. Wiederkommend
Nach drei Monaten, verbracht mit weiteren Studien
Freilich immer noch behindert durch die Unkenntnis der
  neuen Sprache
Bekam er diesmal die Frage vorgelegt: Wer
War der General, der im Bürgerkrieg siegte? Seine Antwort war:
1492. (Laut und freundlich erteilt.) Wieder weggeschickt
Und ein drittes Mal wiederkommend, beantwortete er
Eine dritte Frage: Für wie viele Jahre wird der Präsident gewählt?
Wieder mit: 1492. Nun
Erkannte der Richter, dem der Mann gefiel, daß er die neue
  Sprache

Mad thoughts, gleaming vehicles in which
Jolly-looking people come from nowhere and are nowhere bound.
And houses, built for happy people, therefore standing empty
Even when lived in.

The houses in Hell, too, are not all ugly.
But the fear of being thrown on the street
Wears down the inhabitants of the villas no less than
The inhabitants of the shanty towns.

Translated by Nicholas Jacobs

THE DEMOCRATIC JUDGE

In Los Angeles, before the judge who examines people
Trying to become citizens of the United States
Came an Italian restaurant keeper. After grave preparations
Hindered, though, by his ignorance of the new language
In the test he replied to the question:
What is the 8th Amendment? falteringly:
1492. Since the law demands that applicants know the
    language
He was refused. Returning
After three months spent on further studies
Yet hindered still by ignorance of the new language
He was confronted this time with the question: Who was
The victorious general in the Civil War? His answer was:
1492. (Given amiably, in a loud voice). Sent away again
And returning a third time, he answered
A third question: For how long a term are our Presidents
    elected?
Once more with: 1492. Now
The judge, who liked the man, realised that he could not
Learn the new language, asked him
How he earned his living and was told: by hard work. And so

Nicht lernen konnte, erkundigte sich
Wie er lebte, und erfuhr: schwer arbeitend. Und so
Legte ihm der Richter beim vierten Erscheinen die Frage vor:
Wann
Wurde Amerika entdeckt: Und auf Grund seiner richtigen Antwort
1492, erhielt er die Bürgerschaft.

KINDERKREUZZUG

In Polen, im Jahr Neununddreißig
War eine blutige Schlacht
Die hatte viele Städte und Dörfer
Zu einer Wildnis gemacht.

Die Schwester verlor den Bruder
Die Frau den Mann im Heer;
Zwischen Feuer und Trümmerstätte
Fand das Kind die Eltern nicht mehr.

Aus Polen ist nichts mehr gekommen
Nicht Brief noch Zeitungsbericht.
Doch in den östlichen Ländern
Läuft eine seltsame Geschicht.

Schnee fiel, als man sich's erzählte
In einer östlichen Stadt
Von einem Kinderkreuzzug
Der in Polen begonnen hat.

Da trippelten Kinder hungernd
In Trüpplein hinab die Chausseen
Und nahmen mit sich andere, die
In zerschossenen Dörfern stehn.

At his fourth appearance the judge gave him the question:
When
Was America discovered? And on the strength of his
  correctly answering
1492, he was granted his citizenship.

> *Translated by Michael Hamburger*

CHILDREN'S CRUSADE

In 'thirty-nine in Poland
There was a bloody fight
And many a town and village
Turned to waste land overnight.

Sisters lost their brothers
Wives were widowed by the war
And in fire and desolation
Children found their kin no more.

There came no news from Poland
Neither letter nor printed word
But in an eastern country
A curious tale is heard.

Snow fell, as they related
In a certain eastern town
How a new crusade of children
In Poland had begun.

For all along the highways
Troops of hungry children roamed
And gathered to them others
Who stood by ruined homes.

Sie wollten entrinnen den Schlachten
Dem ganzen Nachtmahr
Und eines Tages kommen
In ein Land, wo Frieden war.

Da war ein kleiner Führer
Das hat sie aufgericht'.
Er hatte eine große Sorge:
Den Weg, den wußte er nicht.

Eine Elfjährige schleppte
Ein Kind von vier Jahr
Hatte alles für eine Mutter
Nur nicht ein Land, wo Frieden war.

Ein kleiner Jude marschierte im Trupp
Mit einem samtenen Kragen
Der war das weißeste Brot gewohnt
Und hat sich gut geschlagen.

Und ging ein dünner Grauer mit
Hielt sich abseits in der Landschaft.
Er trug an einer schrecklichen Schuld:
Er kam aus einer Nazigesandtschaft.

Und da war ein Hund
Gefangen zum Schlachten
Mitgenommen als Esser
Weil sie's nicht übers Herz brachten.

Da war eine Schule
Und ein kleiner Lehrer für Kalligraphie.
Und ein Schüler an einer zerschossenen Tankwand
Lernte schreiben bis zu Frie . . .

Da war auch eine Liebe.
Sie war zwölf, er war fünfzehn Jahr.

They wished to flee the slaughter
For the nightmare did not cease
And some day reach a country
Where there was peace.

They had a little leader
To show them where to go.
Yet he was sorely troubled
Since the way he did not know.

A girl of ten was carrying
A little child of four.
All she lacked to be a mother
Was a country without war.

In a coat with a velvet collar
A little Jew was dressed
He had been reared on whitest bread
But he marched on with the rest.

There was a thin and wretched boy
Who held himself apart.
That he came from a Nazi legation
Was a load of guilt in his heart.

They also had a dog with them
Which they had caught for food.
They spared it; so, another mouth
It followed where it would.

There was a school for penmanship
And teaching did not cease.
On the broken side of a tank
They learned to spell out *peace*.

A girl of twelve, a boy of fifteen
Had a love affair

In einem zerschossenen Hofe
Kämmte sie ihm sein Haar.

Die Liebe konnte nicht bestehen
Es kam zu große Kält:
Wie sollen die Bäumchen blühen
Wenn so viel Schnee drauf fällt?

Da war auch ein Begräbnis
Eines Jungen mit samtenem Kragen
Der wurde von zwei Deutschen
Und zwei Polen zu Grab getragen.

Protestant, Katholik und Nazi war da
Ihn der Erde einzuhändigen.
Und zum Schluß sprach ein kleiner Kommunist
Von der Zukunft der Lebendigen.

So gab es Glaube und Hoffnung
Nur nicht Fleisch und Brot.
Und keiner schelt sie mir, wenn sie was stahln
Der ihnen nicht Obdach bot.

Und keiner schelt mir den armen Mann
Der sie nicht zu Tische lud:
Für ein halbes Hundert, da braucht es
Mehl, nicht Opfermut.

Sie zogen vornehmlich nach Süden.
Süden ist, wo die Sonn
Mittags um zwölf steht
Gradaus davon.

Sie fanden zwar einen Soldaten
Verwundet im Tannengries.

And in a ruined farmyard
She sat and combed his hair.

But love could not endure
Cold wind began to blow:
And how can saplings bloom
When covered deep in snow?

They had a funeral besides
Two Poles and two Germans carried
The boy with the velvet collar
To the place where he was buried.

There were Catholics and Protestants
And Nazis at the grave
At the end a little Communist spoke
Of the future the living have.

So there was faith and hope
But the lack of bread and meat.
And if they stole let no one blame
Who never bade them eat.

Let no one blame the poor man
Who never asked them in
For many have the will but have
No flour in the bin.

They strove to travel southward.
The south is where, 'tis said
At high noon the sun stands
Directly overhead.

They found a wounded soldier
In a pinewood one day.

Sie pflegten ihn sieben Tage
Damit er den Weg ihnen wies.

Er sagte ihnen: Nach Bilgoray!
Muß stark gefiebert haben
Und starb ihnen weg am achten Tag.
Sie haben auch ihn begraben.

Und da gab es ja Wegweiser
Wenn auch vom Schnee verweht
Nur zeigten sie nicht mehr die Richtung an
Sondern waren umgedreht.

Das war nicht etwa ein schlechter Spaß
Sondern aus militärischen Gründen.
Und als sie suchten nach Bilgoray
Konnten sie es nicht finden.

Sie standen um ihren Führer.
Der sah in die Schneeluft hinein
Und deutete mit der kleinen Hand
Und sagte: Es muß dort sein.

Einmal, nachts, sahen sie ein Feuer
Da gingen sie nicht hin.
Einmal rollten drei Tanks vorbei
Da waren Menschen drin.

Einmal kamen sie an eine Stadt
Da machten sie einen Bogen.
Bis sie daran vorüber waren
Sind sie nur nachts weitergezogen.

Wo einst das südöstliche Polen war
Bei starkem Schneewehn

And for a week they tended him
In hopes he'd know the way.

To Bilgoray, he said to them.
The fever made him rave.
Upon the eighth day he died.
They laid him in his grave.

Sometimes there were signposts
Though covered up in snow
All turned around and pointing wrong
But this they did not know.

And no grim joke it was, but done
On military grounds.
And long they sought for Bilgoray
Which never could be found.

They stood about their leader.
Who stared at the snowy sky.
He pointed with his finger
Saying: Yonder it must lie.

Once, at night, they saw a fire
They turned away in fear.
Once three tanks came rolling by
Which meant that men were near.

Once, when they reached a city
They veered and went around.
They traveled then by night alone
Till they had passed the town.

Towards what was south-east Poland
In deeply drifting snow

Hat man die fünfundfünfzig
Zuletzt gesehn.

Wenn ich die Augen schließe
Seh ich sie wandern
Von einem zerschossenen Bauerngehöft
Zu einem zerschossenen andern.

Über ihnen, in den Wolken oben
Seh ich andre Züge, neue, große!
Mühsam wandernd gegen kalte Winde
Heimatlose, Richtungslose

Suchend nach dem Land mit Frieden
Ohne Donner, ohne Feuer
Nicht wie das, aus dem sie kamen
Und der Zug wird ungeheuer.

Und er scheint mir durch den Dämmer
Bald schon gar nicht mehr derselbe:
Andere Gesichtlein seh ich
Spanische, französische, gelbe!

In Polen, in jenem Januar
Wurde ein Hund gefangen
Der hatte um seinen mageren Hals
Eine Tafel aus Pappe hangen.

Darauf stand: Bitte um Hilfe!
Wir wissen den Weg nicht mehr.
Wir sind fünfundfünfzig
Der Hund führt euch her.

Wenn ihr nicht kommen könnt
Jagt ihn weg.

The five and fifty children
Were last seen to go.

And if I close my eyes
I see them wander on
From one ruined barnyard
To another one.

Above them in the clouds I see
A new and greater host
Wearily breasting the cold wind
Homeless and lost

Seeking for a land of peace
Without the crash and flame of war
That scars the soil from which they came
And this host is always more.

Now in the gloom it seems to me
They come from many other places:
In the changing clouds I see
Spanish, French, yellow faces.

In January of that year
Poles caught a hungry dog
Around whose neck a placard hung
'Twas tied there with a cord.

These words thereon were: Please send help!
We don't know where we are.
We are five and fifty
The dog will lead you here.

And if you cannot come to us
Please drive him out.

Schießt nicht auf ihn
Nur er weiß den Fleck.

Die Schrift war eine Kinderhand.
Bauern haben sie gelesen.
Seitdem sind eineinhalb Jahre um.
Der Hund ist verhungert gewesen.

DIE MASKE DES BÖSEN

An meiner Wand hängt ein japanisches Holzwerk
Maske eines bösen Dämons, bemalt mit Goldlack.
Mitfühlend sehe ich
Die geschwollenen Stirnadern, andeutend
Wie sehr es anstrengt, böse zu sein.

Don't shoot the dog for no one else
Can find the spot.

A childish hand had written
The words the peasants read.
Since that time two years have passed.
The starving dog is dead.

Translated by H. R. Hays

THE MASK OF EVIL

On my wall hangs a Japanese carving
The mask of an evil demon, decorated with gold lacquer.
Sympathetically I observe
The swollen veins of the forehead, indicating
What a strain it is to be evil.

Translated by H. R. Hays

From *Poems* Written between 1947 and 1956

Bertolt Brecht

AUF EINEN CHINESISCHEN THEEWURZELLÖWEN

Die Schlechten fürchten deine Klaue.
Die Guten freuen sich deiner Grazie.
Derlei
Hörte ich gern
Von meinem Vers.

DER RADWECHSEL

Ich sitze am Straßenhang.
Der Fahrer wechselt das Rad.
Ich bin nicht gern, wo ich herkomme.
Ich bin nicht gern, wo ich hinfahre.
Warum sehe ich den Radwechsel
Mit Ungeduld?

DIE LÖSUNG

Nach dem Aufstand des 17. Juni
Ließ der Sekretär des Schriftstellerverbands
In der Stalinallee Flugblätter verteilen
Auf denen zu lesen war, daß das Volk
Das Vertrauen der Regierung verscherzt habe
Und es nur durch verdoppelte Arbeit
Zurückerobern könne. Wäre es da
Nicht doch einfacher, die Regierung
Löste das Volk auf und
Wählte ein anderes?

ON A CHINESE CARVING OF A LION

The bad fear your claws.
The good enjoy your elegance.
This
I would like to hear said
Of my verse.

Team Translation

CHANGING THE WHEEL

I sit by the roadside
The driver changes the wheel.
I do not like the place I have come from.
I do not like the place I am going to.
Why with impatience do I
Watch him changing the wheel?

Translated by Michael Hamburger

THE SOLUTION

After the uprising of the 17th June
The Secretary of the Writers' Union
Had leaflets distributed in the Stalinallee
Stating that the people
Had forfeited the confidence of the government
And could win it back only
By redoubled efforts. Would it not be easier
In that case for the government
To dissolve the people
And elect another?

Translated by Derek Bowman

DER RAUCH

Das kleine Haus unter Bäumen am See
Vom Dach steigt Rauch
Fehlte er
Wie trostlos dann wären
Haus, Bäume und See.

THE SMOKE

The little house among trees by the lake.
From the roof smoke rises.
Without it
How dreary would be
House, trees and lake.

Translated by Derek Bowman

Postlude

ALLES WANDELT SICH

Alles wandelt sich. Neu beginnen
Kannst du mit dem letzten Atemzug.
Aber was geschehen, ist geschehen. Und das Wasser
Das du in den Wein gossest, kannst du
Nicht mehr herausschütten.

Was geschehen, ist geschehen. Das Wasser
Das du in den Wein gossest, kannst du
Nicht mehr herausschütten, aber
Alles wandelt sich. Neu beginnen
Kannst du mit dem letzten Atemzug.

EVERYTHING CHANGES

Everything changes. You can make
A fresh start with your final breath.
But what has happened has happened. And the water
You once poured into the wine cannot be
Drained off again.

What has happened has happened. The water
You once poured into the wine cannot be
Drained off again, but
Everything changes. You can make
A fresh start with your final breath.

Translated by John Willett

Part 2
Prose

From *Tales from the Calendar*

SOCRATES WOUNDED

Socrates, the midwife's son, who was able in his dialogues to deliver his friends of well-proportioned thoughts so soundly and easily and with such hearty jests, thus providing them with children of their own, instead of, like other teachers, foisting bastards on them, was considered not only the cleverest of all Greeks but also one of the bravest. His reputation for bravery strikes us as quite justified when we read in Plato how coolly and unflinchingly he drained the hemlock which the authorities offered him in the end for services rendered to his fellow-citizens. Some of his admirers, however, have felt the need to speak of his bravery in the field as well. It is a fact that he fought at the battle of Delium, and this in the light infantry, since neither his standing, a cobbler's, nor his income, a philosopher's, entitled him to enter the more distinguished and expensive branches of the service. Nevertheless, as you may suppose, his bravery was of a special kind.

On the morning of the battle Socrates had primed himself as best he could for the bloody business by chewing onions which, in the soldiers' view, induced valour. His scepticism in many spheres led to credulity in many others; he was against speculative thought and in favour of practical experience; so he did not believe in the gods, but he did believe in onions.

Unfortunately he felt no real effect, at least no immediate one, and so he traipsed glumly in a detachment of swordsmen who were marching in single file to take up their position in a stubble field somewhere. Behind and ahead stumbled Athenian boys from the suburbs, who pointed out that the shields from the Athenian arsenals were too small for fat people like him. He had been thinking the same thing, but in terms of *broad* people who were less than half covered by the absurdly narrow shields.

The exchange of views between the man in front of him and the man behind on the profits made by the big armourers out of small shields was cut short by the order: "Fall out."

They dropped on to the stubble and a captain reprimanded Socrates for trying to sit on his shield. He was less upset by the reprimand than by the hushed voice in which it was given. Apparently the enemy were thought to be near.

The milky morning haze completely obscured the view. Yet the noise of tramping and of clanking arms indicated that the plain was peopled.

With great disquiet Socrates remembered a conversation he had had the previous evening with a fashionable young man whom he had once met behind the scenes and who was a cavalry officer.

"A capital plan!" the young puppy had explained. "The infantry just waits drawn up, loyal and steadfast, and takes the brunt of the enemy's attack. And meanwhile the cavalry advances in the valley and falls on him from the rear."

The valley must lie fairly far to the right, somewhere in the mist. No doubt the cavalry was advancing there now.

The plan had struck Socrates as good, or at any rate not bad. After all, plans were always made, particularly when your strength was inferior to the enemy's. When it came to brass tacks, it was simply a matter of fighting, that is, slashing away. And there was no advance according to plan, but merely according to where the enemy let you.

Now, in the grey dawn, the plan struck Socrates as altogether wretched. What did it mean: the infantry takes the enemy's attack? Usually one was glad to evade an attack, now, all of a sudden, the art lay in taking the brunt of it. A very bad thing that the general himself was a cavalryman.

The ordinary man would need more onions than there were on the market.

And how unnatural it was, instead of lying in bed, to be sitting here on the bare ground in the middle of a field so early in the morning, carrying at least ten pounds of iron about your person and a butcher's knife in your hand. It was quite right to defend the city if it was attacked, for otherwise you would be exposed to gross inconveniences; but why was the city attacked? Because the shipowners, vineyard proprietors and slave-traders in Asia Minor had put a spoke in the wheel of Persian shipowners, vineyard proprietors and slave-traders. A fine reason!

Suddenly everyone sat up.

Through the mist on the left came a muffled roar accompanied by the clang of metal. It spread fairly rapidly. The enemy's attack had begun.

The detachment stood up. With bulging eyes they stared into the mist before them. Ten paces away a man fell on his knees and gibbered an appeal to the gods. Too late, in Socrates' view.

All at once, as if in answer, a fearful roar issued from further to the right. The cry for help seemed to have merged into a death-cry. Socrates saw a little iron rod come flying out of the mist. A javelin.

And then massive shapes, indistinct in the haze, appeared in front: the enemy.

Socrates, with an overpowering sense that perhaps he had already waited too long, turned about awkwardly and took to his heels. His breastplate and heavy greaves hampered him a good deal. They were far more dangerous than shields, because you could not throw them away.

Panting, the philosopher ran across the stubble. Everything depended on whether he could get a good enough start. If only the brave lads behind him were taking the attack for a bit.

Suddenly a fiendish pain shot through him. His left sole stung till he felt he simply could not bear it. Groaning, he sank to the ground, but leapt up again with another yell of pain. With frantic eyes he looked about him and realised what was up. He had landed in a field full of thorns.

There was a tangle of low undergrowth with sharp thorns. A thorn must have stuck in his foot. Carefully, with streaming eyes, he searched for a spot on the ground where he could sit down. He hobbled a few steps in a circle on his sound foot before lowering himself for the second time. He must pull the thorn out at once.

He listened intently to the noise of battle: it extended pretty far on both sides, though straight ahead it was at least a hundred paces away. However, it seemed to be coming nearer, slowly but unmistakably.

Socrates could not get his sandal off. The thorn had pierced the thin leather sole and was deeply embedded in his flesh. How dared they supply soldiers, who were supposed to defend their country against the enemy, with such thin shoes? Each tug at the sandal was attended by searing pain. Exhausted, the poor man's massive shoulders drooped. What now?

His dejected eye fell on the sword at his side. A thought flashed through his mind, more welcome than any that ever came to him in debate. Couldn't the sword be used as a knife? He grabbed it.

At that moment he heard heavy footsteps. A small squad broke through the scrub. Thank the gods, they were his own side! They halted for a few seconds when they saw him. "That's the cobbler," he heard them say. Then they went on.

But now there was a noise from the left too. And there orders in a foreign language rang out. The Persians!

Socrates tried to get to his feet again, that is, to his right foot. He leaned on his sword, which was only a little too short. And then, to the left, in the small clearing, he saw a cluster of men locked in combat. He heard heavy groans and the impact of dull iron on iron or leather.

Desperately he hopped backwards on his sound foot. Twisting it he came down on the injured one and dropped with a moan. When the battling cluster—it was not large, a matter of perhaps twenty or thirty men—had approached to within a few paces, the philosopher was sitting on his backside between two briars looking helplessly at the enemy.

It was impossible for him to move. Anything was better than to feel that pain in the ball of his foot even once more. He did not know what to do and suddenly he started to bellow.

To be precise it was like this: he heard himself bellowing. He heard his voice roaring from the mighty barrel of his thorax: "Over here, Third Battalion! Let them have it, lads!"

And simultaneously he saw himself gripping the sword and swinging it round him in a circle, for in front of him, appearing from the scrub, stood a Persian soldier with a spear. The spear was knocked sideways, tearing the man down with it.

And Socrates heard himself bellowing again and saying:

"Not another step back, lads! Now we've got them where we want them, the sons of bitches! Crapolus, bring up the Sixth! Nullus, to the right! If anyone retreats I'll tear him to shreds!"

To his surprise he saw two of his own side standing by gaping at him in terror. "Roar!" he said softly, "for heaven's sake, roar!" One of them let his jaw drop with fright, but the other actually started roaring something. And the Persian in front of them got up painfully and ran into the brush.

A dozen exhausted men came stumbling out of the clearing. The yelling had made the Persians turn tail. They feared an ambush.

"What's going on here?" one of his fellow-countrymen asked Socrates, who was still sitting on the ground.

"Nothing," he said. "Don't stand about like that gaping at me. You'd better run to and fro giving orders, then they won't realise how few we are."

"We'd better retreat," said the man hesitantly.

"Not one step!" Socrates protested. "Have you got cold feet?"

And as a soldier needs to have not only fear, but also luck, they suddenly heard from some way off, but quite clearly, the trampling of horses and wild shouts, and these were in Greek! Everyone knows how overwhelmingly the Persians were routed that day. It finished the war.

As Alcibiades at the head of the cavalry reached the field of brambles, he saw a group of foot soldiers carrying a stout man shoulder high.

Reining in his horse, he recognised Socrates, and the soldiers told him how, by his unflinching resistance, he had made the wavering battle-line stand firm.

They bore him in triumph to the baggage-train. There, despite his protests, he was put on one of the forage wagons and, surrounded by soldiers streaming with sweat and shouting excitedly, he made his return to the capital.

He was carried shoulder high to his little house.

Xantippe, his wife, made bean soup for him. Kneeling at the hearth and blowing at the fire with puffed out cheeks, she glanced at him from time to time. He was still sitting on the chair where his comrades had set him down.

"What's the matter with *you*?" she asked suspiciously.

"Me?" he muttered, "nothing."

"What's all this talk about your heroic deeds?" she wanted to know.

"Exaggeration," he said. "It smells first class."

"How can it smell when I haven't got the fire going yet? I suppose you've made a fool of yourself again," she said angrily. "And tomorrow when I go for the bread I shall find myself a laughing-stock again."

"I've not made a fool of myself at all. I gave battle."

"Were you drunk?"

"No. I made them stand firm when they were retreating."

"You can't even stand firm yourself," she said, getting up, for the fire had caught. "Pass me the salt-cellar from the table."

"I'm not sure," he said slowly and reflectively, "I'm not sure if I wouldn't prefer on the whole not to eat anything. My stomach's a little upset."

"Just as I said; you're drunk. Try standing up and walking about the room a bit. We'll soon see."

Her unfairness exasperated him. But in no circumstances did he intend to stand up and show her that he could not put his foot to the ground. She was uncannily sharp when it came to nosing out something discreditable to him. And it would be discreditable if the underlying reason for his steadfastness in battle came to light.

She went on busying herself round the stove with the pot and in between let him know her mind.

"I haven't any doubt that your fine friends found you some funk-hole again, well in the rear, near the cookhouse. It's all a fiddle."

In torment he looked out of the little window on to the street where a lot of people with white lanterns were strolling about, for the victory was being celebrated.

His grand friends had tried to do nothing of the sort, nor would he have agreed to it; at all events, not straight off.

"Or did they think it quite in order for the cobbler to march in the ranks? They won't lift a finger for you. He's a cobbler, they say, and let him stay a cobbler. Otherwise we shouldn't be able to visit him in his filthy dump and jabber with him for hours on end and hear the whole world say: what do you think of that, he may be a cobbler, but these grand people sit about with him and talk philersophy. Filthy lot!"

"It's called philerphoby," he said equably.

She gave him an unfriendly look.

"Don't keep on correcting me. I know I'm uneducated. If I weren't you wouldn't have anybody to bring you a tub of water now and again to wash your feet."

He winced and hoped she had not noticed it. On no account must there be any question of washing his feet today. Thank the gods, she was off again on her harangue.

"Well, if you weren't drunk and they didn't find a funk-hole for you either, then you must have behaved like a butcher. So there's blood on your hands, eh? But if I squash a spider, you start shouting. Not that I believe you really fought like a man, but you must have done something crafty, something a bit underhand or they wouldn't be slapping you on the back like this. I'll find out sooner or later, don't you worry."

The soup was now ready. It smelled enticing. The woman took the pot and, holding the handles with her skirt, set it on the table and began to ladle it out.

He wondered whether, after all, he had not better recover his appetite. The thought that he would then have to go to the table restrained him just in time.

He did not feel at all easy. He was well aware that the last word had not yet been said. There was bound to be a lot of unpleasantness before long. You could hardly decide a battle against the Persians and be left in peace. At the moment, in the first flush of victory, no one, of course, gave a thought to the man responsible for it. Everyone was fully occupied proclaiming his own glorious deeds from the housetops. But tomorrow or the day after, everyone would wake up to the fact that the other fellow was claiming all the credit, and then they would be anxious to push him forward. So many would be able to score off so many others if the cobbler were proclaimed the real hero in chief. They couldn't stand Alcibiades as it was. What pleasure it would give them to throw in his teeth: Yes, you won the battle, but a cobbler fought it.

And the thorn hurt more savagely than ever. If he did not get his sandal off soon, it might mean blood-poisoning.

"Don't smack your lips like that," he said absentmindedly.

The spoon remained stuck in his wife's mouth.

"Don't do what?"

"Nothing," he hastened to assure her in alarm. "I was miles away."

She stood up, beside herself, banged the pot down on the stove and went out.

He heaved a deep sigh of relief. Hastily he levered himself out of the chair and hopped to his couch at the back, looking round nervously. As she came back to fetch her wrap to go out she looked suspiciously at the way he lay motionless on the leather-covered hammock. For a moment she thought there must be something the matter with him after all. She even considered asking him, for she was very devoted to him. But she thought better of it and left the room sulkily to watch the festivities with the woman from next door.

Socrates slept badly and restlessly and woke up feeling worried. He had got his sandal off, but had not been able to get hold of the thorn. His foot was badly swollen.

His wife was less sharp than usual this morning.

She had heard the whole city talking about her husband the evening before. Something really must have happened to impress people so deeply. That he had held up an entire Persian battle-line she certainly could not accept. Not him, she told herself. Yes, hold up an entire public meeting with his questions, he could do that all right. But not a battle-line. So what had happened?

She was so uncertain that she brought him in goat's milk in bed. He made no attempt to get up.

"Aren't you going out?" she asked.

"Don't feel like it," he growled.

That is not the way to answer a civil question from your wife, but she thought that perhaps he only wanted to avoid being stared at and let the answer pass.

Visitors began arriving early: a few young men, the sons of well-off parents, his usual associates. They always treated him as their teacher and some of them even made notes while he talked, as though it were something quite special.

Today they told him at once that Athens resounded with his fame. It was an historic date for philosophy (so she had been right after all: it was called philersophy and not something else). Socrates had demonstrated, they said, that the great thinker could also be the great man of action.

Socrates listened to them without his usual mockery. As they spoke he seemed to hear, still far away, as one hears a distant thunderstorm, stupendous laughter, the laughter of a whole city, even of a whole country, far away, but drawing nearer, irresistibly approaching, infecting everyone: the passersby in the streets, the merchants and politicians in the marketplace, the artisans in their little workshops.

"That's all rubbish what you're saying," he said with a sudden resolve. "I didn't do anything at all."

They looked at each other and smiled. Then one of them said:

"That's just what we said. We knew you'd take it like that. What's this hullabaloo all of a sudden, we asked Eusopulos outside the gymnasium. For ten years Socrates had been performing the greatest intellectual feats and no one so much as turned his head to look at him. Now he's won a battle and the whole of Athens is talking about him. Don't you see how disgraceful it is, we said."

Socrates groaned.

"But I didn't win it at all. I defended myself because I was attacked. I wasn't interested in this battle. I never trade in arms nor do I own vineyards in the area. I wouldn't know what to fight battles for. I found myself among a lot of sensible men from the suburbs, who have no interest in battles, and I did exactly what they all did, at the most, a few seconds before them."

They were dumbfounded.

"There you are!" they exclaimed, "that's what we said too. He did nothing but defend himself. That's his way of winning battles. With your permission we'll hurry back to the gymnasium. We interrupted a discussion on this subject only to wish you good morning."

And off they went, in deeply savoured discussion.

Socrates lay propped up in his elbows in silence and gazed at the smoke-blackened ceiling. His gloomy forebodings had been right.

His wife watched him from a corner of the room. Mechanically she went on mending an old dress.

All of a sudden she asked softly: "Well, what's behind it all?"

He gave a start. He looked at her uncertainly.

She was a worn-out creature, flat-chested as a board and sad-eyed. He knew he could depend on her. She would still be standing up for him when his pupils would be saying: "Socrates? Isn't that the vile cobbler who repudiates the gods?" He'd been a bad bargain for her, but she did not complain—except to him. And there had never yet been an evening without some bread and a bit of bacon for him on the shelf when he came home hungry from his rich pupils.

He wondered whether he should tell her everything. But then he realised that before long, when people, like those just now, came to see him and talked about his heroic deeds, he would have to utter a whole lot of lies and hypocrisies in her hearing, and he could not bring himself to do that if she knew the truth, for he respected her.

So he let it be and just said: "Yesterday's cold bean soup is stinking the whole place out again."

She only shot him another suspicious look.

Naturally they were in no position to throw food away. He was only trying to find something to sidetrack her. Her conviction that there was something wrong with him grew. Why didn't he get up? He always got up late, but simply because he went to bed late. Yesterday he had gone to bed very early. And today, with victory celebrations, the whole city was on the go. All the shops in the street were shut. Some of the cavalry that had been pursuing the enemy had got back at five o'clock this morning, the clatter of horses' hoofs had been heard. He adored tumultuous crowds. On occasions like this he ran round from morning till night, getting into conversation with people. So why wasn't he getting up?

The threshold darkened and in came four officials. They remained standing in the middle of the room and one of them said in a businesslike but exceedingly respectful tone that he was instructed to escort Socrates to the Areopagus. The general, Alcibiades himself, had proposed that a tribute be paid to him for his martial feats.

A hum of voices from the street showed that the neighbours were gathering outside the house.

Socrates felt sweat breaking out. He knew that now he would have to get up and, even if he refused to go with them, he would at least have to get on his feet, say something polite and accompany these men to the door. And he knew that he would not be able to take more than two steps at the most. Then they would look at his foot and know what was up. And the enormous laughter would break out, there and then.

So, instead of getting up, he sank back on his hard pillow and said cantankerously:

"I require no tribute. Tell the Areopagus that I have an appointment with some friends at eleven o'clock to thrash out a philosophical question that interests us, and therefore, much to my regret, I cannot come. I am altogether unfitted for public functions and feel much too tired."

This last he added because he was annoyed at having dragged in philosophy, and the first part he said because he hoped that rudeness was the easiest way to shake them off.

The officials certainly understood this language. They turned on their heels and left, treading on the feet of the people standing outside.

"One of these days they'll teach you to be polite to the authorities," said his wife angrily and went into the kitchen.

Socrates waited till she was outside. Then he swiftly swung his heavy body round in the bed, seated himself on the edge of it, keeping a wary eye on the door, and tried with infinite caution to step on the bad foot. It seemed hopeless.

Streaming with sweat he lay back again.

Half an hour passed. He took up a book and read. So long as he kept his foot still he felt practically nothing.

Then his friend Antisthenes turned up.

He did not remove his heavy coat, remained standing at the foot of the couch, coughed in a rather forced way and scratched his throat with its bristly beard as he looked at Socrates.

"Still in bed? I thought I should only find Xantippe at home. I got up specially to enquire after you. I had a bad cold and that was why I couldn't come along yesterday."

"Sit down," said Socrates monosyllabically.

Antisthenes fetched a chair from the corner and sat down by his friend.

"I'm starting the lessons again tonight. No reason to interrupt them any longer."

"No."

"Of course, I wondered whether they'd turn up. Today there are the great banquets. But on the way here I ran into young Phaeston and when I told him that I was taking algebra tonight, he was simply delighted. I told him he could come in his helmet. Protagoras and the others will hit the ceiling with rage when it's known that on the night after the battle they just went on studying algebra at Antisthenes'."

Socrates rocked himself gently in his hammock, pushing himself off the slightly crooked wall with the flat of his hand. His protuberant eyes looked searchingly at his friend.

"Did you meet anybody else?"

"Heaps of people."

Socrates gazed sourly at the ceiling. Should he make a clean breast of it to Antisthenes? He felt pretty sure of him. He himself never took money for lessons and was therefore not in competition with Antisthenes. Perhaps he really ought to lay the difficult case before him.

Antisthenes looked with his sparkling cricket's eyes inquisitively at his friend and told him:

"Giorgius is going about telling everyone that you must have been on the run and in the confusion gone the wrong way, that's to say, forward. A few of the more decent young people want to thrash him for it."

Unpleasantly surprised, Socrates looked at him.

"Rubbish," he said with annoyance. He realized in a flash what trumps his opponents would hold if he declared himself.

During the night, towards morning, he had wondered whether he might not present the whole thing as an experiment and say he had wanted to see just how gullible people were. "For twenty years I've been teaching pacifism in every back street, and one rumour was enough for my own pupils to take me for a berserker," and so on and so on. But then the battle ought not to have been won. Patently this was an unfavourable moment for pacifism. After a defeat even the top dogs were pacifists for a while; after a victory even the underdogs approved of war, at any rate for a while, until they noticed that for them there wasn't all that difference between victory and defeat. No, he couldn't cut much ice with pacifism just now.

There was a clatter of horses in the street. The riders halted in front of the house and in came Alcibiades with his buoyant step.

"Good morning, Antisthenes, how's the philosophy business going? They're in a great state," he cried, beaming. "There's an uproar in the Areopagus over your answer, Socrates. As a joke I've changed my proposal to give you a laurel wreath to the proposal to give you fifty strokes. Of course, that annoyed them, because it exactly expressed their feelings. But you'll have to come along, you know. We'll go together, on foot."

Socrates sighed. He was on very good terms with young Alcibiades. They had often drunk together. It was very nice of him to call. It was certainly not only his wish to rile the Areopagus. And that wish itself was an honourable one and deserved every support.

At last he said cautiously as he went on rocking himself in his hammock: "Haste is the wind that blows the scaffolding down. Take a seat."

Alcibiades laughed and drew up a chair. Before he sat down he bowed politely to Xantippe, who stood at the kitchen door wiping her wet hands on her skirt.

"You philosophers are funny people," he said a little impatiently. "For all I know you may be regretting now that you helped us win the battle. I daresay Antisthenes has pointed out to you that there weren't enough good reasons for it."

"We've been talking about algebra," said Antisthenes quickly and coughed again.

Alcibiades grinned.

"Just as I expected. For heaven's sake, no fuss about a thing of this sort, what? Now to my mind it was sheer bravery. Nothing remarkable, if you like; but what's so remarkable about a handful of laurel leaves? Grit your teeth and go through with it, old man. It'll soon be over, and it won't hurt. And then we can go and have one."

He looked searchingly at the broad powerful figure, which was now rocking rather violently.

Socrates thought fast. He had hit on something that he could say. He could say that he had sprained his foot last night or this morning. When the men had lowered him from their shoulders for instance. There was even a moral to it: the case demonstrated how easily you could come to grief through being honoured by your fellow-citizens.

Without ceasing to swing himself, he leant forward so that he was sitting upright, rubbed his bare left arm with his right hand and said slowly:

"It's like this. My foot . . ."

As he spoke the word his glance, which was not quite steady—for now it was a matter of uttering the first real lie in this affair; so far he had merely kept silence—fell upon Xantippe at the kitchen door.

Socrates' speech failed him. All of a sudden he no longer wanted to produce his tale. His foot was not sprained.

The hammock came to a standstill.

"Listen, Alcibiades," he said forcefully and in a quite different voice, "there can't be any talk of bravery in this matter. As soon as the battle started, that's to say, as soon as I caught sight of the first Persian, I ran for it and, what's more, in the right direction — in retreat. But there was a field full of thorns. I got a thorn in my foot and couldn't go on. Then I laid about me like a savage and almost struck some of our own men. In desperation I yelled something about other units, to make the Persians believe there were some, which was absurd because of course they don't understand Greek. At the same time they seem to have been a bit nervous themselves. I suppose they just couldn't stand the roaring at that stage, after all they'd had to go through during the advance. They stopped short for a moment and at that point our cavalry turned up. That's all."

For a few seconds it was very quiet in the room. Alcibiades stared at him unblinkingly. Antisthenes coughed behind his hand, this time quite naturally. From the kitchen door, where Xantippe was standing, came a loud peal of laughter.

Then Antisthenes said drily:

"And so of course you couldn't go to the Areopagus and limp up the steps to receive the laurel wreath. I can understand that."

Alcibiades leant back in his chair and contemplated the philosopher on the couch with narrowed eyes. Neither Socrates nor Antisthenes looked at him.

He bent forward again and clasped one knee with his hands. His narrow boyish face twitched a little, but it betrayed nothing of his thoughts or feelings.

"Why didn't you say you had some other sort of wound?" he asked.

"Because I've got a thorn in my foot," said Socrates bluntly.

"Oh, that's why?" said Alcibiades. "I see."

He rose swiftly and went up to the bed.

"Pity I didn't bring my own wreath with me. I gave it to my man to hold. Otherwise I should leave it here for you. You can take my word for it, I think you're brave enough. I don't know anybody who in this situation would have told the story you've just told."

And he went out quickly.

As Xantippe was bathing his foot later and extracting the thorn she said acrimoniously:

"It could have meant blood-poisoning."

"Or worse," said the philosopher.

Translated by Yvonne Kapp

THE UNSEEMLY OLD LADY

My grandmother was seventy-two years old when my grandfather died. He had a small lithographer's business in a little town in Baden and there he worked with two or three assistants until his death. My grandmother managed the household without a maid, looked after the ramshackle old house and cooked for the menfolk and children.

She was a thin little woman with lively lizard's eyes, though slow of speech. On very scanty means she had reared five of the seven children she had borne. As a result, she had grown smaller with the years.

Her two girls went to America and two of the sons also moved away. Only the youngest, who was delicate, stayed in the little town. He became a printer and set up a family far too large for him.

So after my grandfather died she was alone in the house.

The children wrote each other letters dealing with the problem of what should be done about her. One of them could offer her a home, and the printer wanted to move with his family into her house. But the old woman turned a deaf ear to these proposals and would only accept, from each of her children who could afford it, a small monetary allowance. The lithographer's business, long behind the times, was sold for practically nothing, and there were debts as well.

The children wrote saying that, all the same, she could not live quite alone, but since she entirely ignored this, they gave in and sent her a little money every month. At any rate, they thought, there was always the printer who had stayed in the town.

What was more, he undertook to give his brothers and sisters news of their mother from time to time. The printer's letters to my father, and what my father himself learnt on a visit and, two years later, after my grandmother's burial, give me a picture of what went on in those two years.

It seems that, from the start, the printer was disappointed that my grandmother had declined to take him into the house, which was fairly large and now standing empty. He had four children and lived in three rooms. But in any case the old lady had only very casual relations with him. She invited the children for coffee every Sunday afternoon, and that was about all.

She visited her son once or twice in three months and helped her daughter-in-law with the jam-making. The young woman gathered from some of her remarks that she found the printer's little dwelling too cramped for her. He, in reporting this, could not forbear to add an exclamation mark.

My father wrote asking what the old woman was up to nowadays, to which he replied rather curtly: going to the cinema.

It must be understood that this was not at all the thing; at least, not in her children's eyes. Thirty years ago the cinema was not what it is today. It meant wretched, ill-ventilated premises, often converted from disused skittle-alleys, with garish posters outside displaying the murders and tragedies of passion. Strictly speaking, only adolescents went or, for the darkness, courting couples. An old woman there by herself would certainly be conspicuous.

And there was another aspect of this cinema-going to be considered. Of course, admission was cheap, but since the pleasure fell more or less into the category of self-indulgences it represented "money thrown away." And to throw money away was not respectable.

Furthermore, not only did my grandmother keep up no regular association with her son in town, but she neither invited nor visited any of her other acquaintances. She never went to the coffee-parties in the little town. On the other hand, she frequented a cobbler's workshop in a poor and even slightly notorious alley where, especially in the afternoon, all manner of none too reputable characters hung about: out-of-work waitresses and itinerant craftsmen. The cobbler was a middle-aged man who had knocked about the world and never made much of himself. It was also said that he drank. In any case, he was no proper associate for my grandmother.

The printer intimated in a letter that he had hinted as much to his mother and had met with a very cool reply. "He's seen a thing or two," she answered and that was the end of the conversation. It was not easy to talk to my grandmother about things she did not wish to discuss.

About six moths after my grandfather's death the printer wrote to my father saying that their mother now ate at the inn every other day.

That really was news! Grandmother, who all her life had cooked for a dozen people and herself had always eaten up the leavings, now ate at the inn. What had come over her?

Shortly after this, my father made a business trip in the neighbourhood and he visited his mother. She was just about to go out when he turned up. She took off her hat again and gave him a glass of red wine and a biscuit. She seemed in a perfectly equable mood, neither particularly animated nor particularly silent. She asked after us, though not in much detail, and wanted principally to know whether there were cherries for the children. There she was quite her old self. The room was of course scrupulously clean and she looked well.

The only thing that gave an indication of her new life was that she did not want to go with my father to the churchyard to visit her husband's grave. "You can go by yourself," she said lightly. "It's the third on the left in the eleventh row. I've got to go somewhere."

The printer said afterwards that probably she had had to go to her cobbler. He complained bitterly.

"Here am I, stuck in this hole with my family and only five hours' badly-paid work, on top of which my asthma's troubling me again, while the house in the main street stands empty."

My father had taken a room at the inn, but nevertheless expected to be invited by his mother, if only as a matter of form; however, she did not mention it. Yet even when the house had been full, she had always objected to his not staying with them and spending money on an hotel into the bargain.

But she appeared to have finished with family life and to be treading new paths now in the evening of her days. My father, who had his fair share of humour, found her "pretty sprightly" and told my uncle to let the old woman do what she wanted.

And what did she want to do?

The next thing reported was that she had hired a brake and taken an excursion on a perfectly ordinary Thursday. A brake was a large, high-sprung, horse-drawn vehicle with a seating capacity for whole families. Very occasionally, when we grandchildren had come for a visit, grandfather had hired a brake. Grandmother had always stayed behind. With a scornful wave of the hand she had refused to come along.

And after the brake came the trip to K., a larger town some two hours' distance by train. There was a race-meeting there and it was to the races that my grandmother went.

The printer was now positively alarmed. He wanted to have a doctor called in. My father shook his head as he read the letter, but was against calling in a doctor.

My grandmother had not travelled alone to K. She had taken with her a young girl who, according to the printer's letter, was slightly feeble-minded: the kitchen-maid at the inn where the old lady took her meals every second day.

From now on this "half-wit" played quite a part.

My grandmother apparently doted on her. She took her to the cinema and to the cobbler—who, incidentally, turned out to be a Social Democrat—and it was rumoured that the two women played cards in the kitchen over a glass of wine.

"Now she's bought the half-wit a hat with roses on it," wrote the printer in despair. "And our Anna has no Communion dress!"

My uncle's letters became quite hysterical, dealt only with the "unseemly behaviour of our dear mother" and otherwise said nothing. The rest I know from my father.

The innkeeper had whispered to him with a wink: "Mrs. B's enjoying herself nowadays, so they say."

As a matter of fact, even in these last years my grandmother did not live extravagantly in any way. When she did not eat at the inn, she usually took no more than a little egg dish, some coffee and, above all, her beloved biscuits. She did, however, allow herself a cheap red wine, of which she drank a small glass at every meal. She kept the house very clean, and not just the bedroom and kitchen which she used. All the same, without her children's knowledge, she mortgaged it. What she did with the money never came out. She seems to have given it to the cobbler. After her death he moved to another town and was said to have started a fair-sized business in handmade shoes.

When you come to think of it, she lived two lives in succession. The first one as a daughter, wife and mother; the second simply as Mrs. B, an unattached person without responsibilities and with modest but sufficient means. The first life lasted some sixty years; the second no more than two.

My father learnt that in the last six months she had permitted herself certain liberties unknown to normal people. Thus she might rise in summer at three in the morning and take walks in the deserted streets of the little town, which she had entirely to herself. And, it was generally alleged, when the priest called on her to keep the old woman company in her loneliness, she invited him to the cinema.

She was not at all lonely. A crowd of jolly people forgathered at the cobbler's, it appears, and there was much gossip. She always kept a bottle of her red wine there and drank her little glassful whilst the others gossiped and inveighed against the town officials. This wine was reserved for her, though sometimes she provided stronger drink for the company.

She died quite suddenly on an autumn afternoon, in her bedroom, though not in bed but on an upright chair by the window. She had invited the "half-wit" to the cinema that evening, so the girl was with her when she died. She was seventy-four years old.

I have seen a photograph of her which was taken for the children and shows her laid out.

What you see is a tiny little face, very wrinkled, and a thin-lipped, wide mouth. Much that is small, but no smallness. She had savoured to the full the long years of servitude and the short years of freedom and consumed the bread of life to the last crumb.

Translated by Yvonne Kapp

Acknowledgments

Every reasonable effort has been made to locate the owners of rights to previously published works and the translations printed here. We gratefully acknowledge permission to reprint the following material:

POETRY, from *Bertolt Brecht, Gesammelte Werke in 20 Bänden.* Frankfurt am Main, 1967. Einzelbände folgen from volumes 2, 8, 9, 10, *Gedichte 1* © 1967, from *Gedichte 2* © 1988. Reproduced by permission of Suhrkamp Verlag.

Prelude, From *Poems* written between 1913 and 1926, From *Poems* written between 1926 and 1933, From *Poems* written between 1933 and 1938, From *Poems* written between 1938 and 1941, From *Poems* written between 1941 and 1947, From *Poems* written between 1947 and 1956, and Postlude, copyright © 1976, 1979 by Methuen Publishing Limited, London. From BERTOLT BRECHT: POEMS 1913-1956, edited by John Willett and Ralph Manheim. Reproduced by permission of Routledge, Inc., and Methuen Publishing Limited, London.

"Socrates Wounded" and "The Unseemly Old Lady," copyright © 1967 by Suhrkamp Verlag, Frankfurt am Main. Geschichten aus Prosa I copyright © by Stefan S. Brecht. Translation copyright © 1983 by Stefan S. Brecht. Published by Arcade Publishing, New York, N.Y. Reproduced by permission of Stefan S. Brecht and Arcade Publishing.

Author Listing in The German Library by Volume Number

Abbe, Ernst 36
Adorno, Theodor W. 43, 61, 78
Aichinger, Ilse 99
Albert, Heinrich 9
Allmers, Hermann 42
Alte, Reinmar der 9
Anonymous: from Carmina Burana 9
Anonymous: Dr. Faust 4
Anonymous: Duke Ernst 4
Anonymous: Muspilli 9
Anonymous: Song of the Nibelunglied 1
Anonymous: The Battle of Ravenna 1
Anonymous: The Older Lay of Hildebrand 1
Anonymous: from Theologia Germanica 5
Anonymous: The Rose Garden 1
Anonymous: The Younger Lay of Hildebrand 1
Anschütz, Ernst 54
Arnim, Achim von 35
Arnim, Bettina von 43
Audorf, Jakob 53
Aue, Hartmann von 4, 9

Bach, Johann Sebastian 51
Bachofen, Johann Jakob 36
Bachmann, Ingeborg 86, 94
Balthasar, H. von 54
Barth, Karl 54
Baumbach, Rudolf 53
Bebel, August 41
Becher, Johannes R. 53
Bechstein, Ludwig 29
Becker, Jürgen 86
Becker, Jurek 87, 99
Beer, Johann 7
Beethoven, Ludwig van 42, 51, 52
Bender, Hans 99
Bendix, Richard 61
Benn, Gottfried 66, 73
Berg, Alban 51
Bernstein, Eduard 41
Bichsel, Peter 99
Bierbaum, Otto Julius 42
Biermann, Wolf 53
Bingen, Hildegard von 5
Birken, Sigmund von 9
Blackenburg, Friedrich von 11
Bloch, Ernst 43
Bobrowski, Johannes 87
Böda-Löhner, Fritz 53

Complete Author Listing in The German Library

Böhme, Jakob 5
Boelitz, Martin 42
Börne, Ludwig 33
Borchert, Wolfgang 86, 99
Bosch, Robert 82
Bräker, Ulrich 10
Bräunig, Werner 87
Brahms, Johannes 51
Brant, Sebastian 6
Brasch, Thomas 99
Braun, Volker 87
Brecht, Bertolt 43, 53, 75, 83, 87
Brehm, Alfred E. 36
Brentano, Clemens, 30, 35, 39, 42
Breuer, Hans 43
Brežan, Jurij 87
Bruchmann, Franz Ritter von 42
Bruckner, Anton 51
de Bruyn, Günter 87
Buber, M. 54
Buch, Hans Christoph 99
Büchner, Georg 28, 83
Bürger, Gottfried August 11, 39
Bultmann, R. 54
Burckhardt, Jacob 36, 49, 79
Busch, Wilhelm 50
Busoni, Ferruccio 51
Butenandt, Adolf 82

Campe, Johann Heinrich 42
Celtis, Conrad 6
Chamisso, Adelbert von 35, 36, 42
Chezy, Helmina von 42
Claudius, Hermann 53
Claudius, Matthias 39, 42, 53
Clausewitz, Carl von 36
Collin, Matthäus von 42
Craigher de Jachelutta, Jakob N. 42
Czerny, Carl 51

Dach, Simon 9, 53
Dahlhaus, Carl 43
Dahrendorf, Ralf 61
Dahn, Daniela 87

Daimler, Gottfried 36
Daumer, Georg Friedrich 42
Degenhardt, Franz Josef 53
Dehmel, Richard 42, 53
Des Knaben Wunderhorn 42
Dessau, Paul 51
Dietzgen, Joseph 41
Dilthey, Wilhelm 49, 62
Disselhoff, August 53
Ditters von Dittersdorf, Karl 51
Döblin, Alfred 68
Dorst, Tankred 83
Drach, Hans 53
Droste-Hülshoff, Annette von 37, 39
Droysen, Johann Gustav 49
Dürrenmatt, Friedrich 83, 89
Dvořák, Max 79

Ebel, Edward 53
Ebner-Eschenbach, Marie von 38
Eckhart, Meister 5
Egk, Werner 51
Ehrlich, Paul 36
Eich, Günter 86
Eichendorff, Joseph Freiherr von 30, 35, 39, 42, 53
Eigen, Manfred 82
Eildermann, Heinrich Arnulf 53
Einstein, Albert 82
Eisler, Hanns 51
Eist, Dietmar von 9
Engels, Friedrich 40, 41, 49, 83
Enzensberger, Hans Magnus 69, 98
Erasmus, Desiderius 6
Erdmann, Georg 51
Ernst, Karl 53
Eschenbach, Wolfram von 9
Euler, Leonhard 36

Falk, Johann Daniel 53
Fetscher, Iring 29
Feuerbach, Ludwig 40, 54
Fichte, Johann Gottlieb 23, 49

Complete Author Listing in The German Library

Fischer, A. 53
Fischer-Dieskau, Dietrich 44
Fleming, Paul 9
Fleißer, Marieluise 58
Fontane, Theodor 46, 47
Forkel, Johann Nikolaus 43
Forster, Georg 10
Fraunhofer, Joseph von 36
Freiligrath, Ferdinand 42, 53
Freud, Anna 62
Freud, Sigmund 54, 59
Freytag, Gustav 83
Fries, Fritz Rudolf 87
Frisch, Max 83, 90
Fröhlich, Hans J. 99
Fromm, Erich 62
Fühmann, Franz 87
Furtwängler, Wilhelm 43

Gandersheim, Hrotsvitha von 8
Gartenaere, Wernher der 4
Gaudenz, J. 53
Gauss, Karl Friedrich 36
Gebhardt, P. 53
Geibel, Emanuel 42, 53
Geiger, Theodor 61
Gellert, Christian Fürchtegott 42
Gerhardt, Paul 9, 53
Gerhardt, Uta 61
Gerth, Hans 61
Gervinus, Georg Gottfried 49
Gilm zu Rosenegg, Hermann von 42
Glaßbrenner, Adolf 53
Gleim, Johann Wilhelm Ludwig 9
Glichezaere, Heinrich der 4
Gluck, Christoph Willibald 51
Gödel, Kurt 82
Görres, Joseph 21
Goethe, Johann Wolfgang von 11, 18, 19, 20, 30, 39, 42, 53, 54, 79, 83
Götz, Johann Nikolaus 9
Goldschmidt, A. 79

Gotthelf, Jeremias 37
Gottsched, Johann Christoph 11
Grass, Günter 93
Greiffenberg, Catharina Regina von 7, 9
Grillparzer, Franz 31, 37, 83
Grimm, Jakob; Wilhelm 21, 29
Grimmelshausen, Hans Jakob C. von 7, 9
Groth, Klaus 42
Gruppe, Otto Friedrich 42
Gryphius, Andreas 8, 9
Grzimek, Martin 99
Günther, Johann Christian 9

Habermas, Jürgen 61
Hacks, Peter 83
Händel, Georg Friedrich 51
Hagedorn, Friedrich von 9
Hahn, Otto 82
Halm, August 43
Halm, Friedrich (Baron Elegius von Münch-Bellinghausen) 42
Hamann, Johann Georg 11
Handke, Peter 83, 86, 100
Hanslick, Eduard 43
Hartmann, Karl Amadeus 51
Hasenclever, Walter 66
Hasse, Johann Adolf 51
Hauff, Wilhelm 30
Hauptmann, Gerhart 38, 57, 83
Hausegger, Friedrich von 43
Hausen, Friedrich von 9
Hauser, Arnold 83
Haydn, Franz Joseph 51
Hebel, Johann Peter 35
Hebbel, Friedrich 31, 39, 83
Hegel, Georg Wilhelm Friedrich 24, 43, 49, 54, 83
Hegel, Max 53
Hein, Christoph 87
Heine, Heinrich 32, 33, 39, 42, 53
Heinse, Wilhelm 10, 79
Heisenberg, Werner 82

Complete Author Listing in The German Library

Helmholtz, Hermann von 36
Henckell, Karl 42
Henze, Hans Werner 51
Herder, Johann Gottfried 11, 43, 49, 53
Hermand, Jost 43
Hermlin, Stephan 87
Herrosee, Carl Friedrich Wilhelm 42
Herwegh, Georg 53
Hesse, Hermann 42, 71
Hetzer, Theodor 79
Hey, Wilhelm 53
Heym, Stefan 87
Heyse, Paul Johann Ludwig 38, 42
Hilbig, Wolfgang 87
Hildesheimer, Wolfgang 83
Hindemith, Paul 51
Hochhuth, Rolf 83, 96
Hölderlin, Friedrich 21, 22, 39
Hölty, Ludwig Christoph Heinrich 39, 42, 53
Hoffmann, E. T. A. 26, 30, 43, 51
Hoffmann, Heinrich August: Hoffmann von Fallersleben 42, 53
Hofmannsthal, Hugo von 30, 83
Hofmannswaldau, Christian Hofmann von 9
Holz, Arno 69, 83
Horkheimer, Max 61, 78
Horváth, Ödön von 58, 83
Hüsch, Hans Dieter 53
Hufeland, Christoph von 36
Humboldt, Alexander von 36
Humboldt, Wilhelm von 21, 86
Husserl, Edmund 62
Hutten, Ulrich von 6, 9

Ihering, Rudolf von 36

Jacobi, Friedrich Heinrich 23
Jahnke, Franz 53
Jaspers, Karl 49, 54, 62
Jean Paul 21, 34
Johannsdorf, Albrecht von 9
Johansen, Hannah 99
Johnson, Uwe 91
Jung, Carl Gustav 62

Kästner, Erich 50
Kafka, Franz 30, 65
Kaiser, Georg 66, 83
Kant, Hermann 87
Kant, Immanuel 13, 43, 49, 54
Kaschnitz, Marie Luise 99
Kautsky, Karl 41
Keller, Gottfried 39, 42, 44
Kerner, Justinus 39, 42
Kipphardt, Heinar 83, 96
Kirsch, Sarah 87
Klaj, Johann 9
Kleber, Leonhard 53
Kleist, Ewald Christian von 9
Kleist, Heinrich von 21, 25, 34, 35
Klinger, Friedrich Maximilian 14
Klopstock, Friedrich Gottlob 9, 11, 42
Knepler, Georg 43
Knobloch, Heinz 87
Koch, Robert 82
König, Barbara 99
König, René 61
Königsdorf, Helga 87
Köpf, Gerhard 99
Kohlhaase, Wolfgang 87
Kokoschka, Oskar 66
Koloff, Eduard 79
Krenek, Ernst 51
Kroetz, Franz Xaver 83, 97
Kürenberg, Der von 9
Kugler, Franz 42
Kuhlmann, Quirinus 9
Kuhnau, Johann 7
Kunze, Reiner 87
Kunert, Günter 87, 99

Complete Author Listing in The German Library

Laabs, Joochen 87
Langhoff, Wolfgang 53
Lappe, Karl 42
La Roche, Sophie von 10
Lassalle, Ferdinand 41
Leander, R. 42
Lederer, Emil 41
Lehne, Friedrich 53
Leibfried, Stephan 61
Leibniz, Gottfried Wilhelm 7
Lenau, Nikolaus 39, 42
Lenz, Jakob Michael Reinhold 11, 14, 83
Lenz, Siegfried 99
Lessing, Gotthold Ephraim 11, 12, 54, 83
Lettau, Reinhard 86, 99
Levy, Julius 53
Lichtenberg, Georg Christoph 36
Liebig, Justus von 36
Liebknecht, Wilhelm 41
Liebmann, Irina 87
Liliencron, Detlev von 42
Lingg, Hermann Ritter von 42
List, Friedrich 36
Liszt, Franz 51
Loest, Erich 87
Loewenstein, Rudolf 53
Logau, Friedrich von 9
Lohenstein, Daniel Casper von 7, 8, 9
Lorenz, Konrad 82
Lotzer, Sebastian 6
Ludwig, Christian Gottlieb 43
Lüchow, J. C. 53
Lukács, Georg 83
Luther, Martin, 6, 9, 53
Luxemburg, Rosa 41

Mach, Ernst 82
Mackay, John Henry 42
Magdeburg, Mechthild von 5
Mahler, Gustav 51
Mann, Heinrich 64

Mann, Thomas 19, 43, 63
Mannheim, Karl 61
Marx, Karl 40, 41, 49, 54, 83
Matthison, Friedrich von 42
Mayer, Günter 43
Mayer, Karl Ulrich 61
Mayntz, Renate 61
Mayrhofer, Johann 42
Mechtel, Angelika 99
Meckel, Christoph 99
Mehring, Franz 41
Meinecke, Friedrich 49
Meitner, Lise 82
Melle, F. Hendrik 87
Mendelssohn, Moses 11
Mendelssohn-Bartholdy, Felix 51
Meyer, Conrad Ferdinand 38, 39
Michels, Robert 61
Moeller, Edith 53
Mörike, Eduard Friedrich 30, 37, 42
Mohr, Joseph 53
Mommsen, Theodor 49
Morgenstern, Beate 87
Morgenstern, Christian 50
Morgner, Irmtraud 87
Moritz, Karl Philipp 10, 11
Morungen, Heinrich von 9
Moscherosch, Johann Michael 7
Mosen, Julius 42
Mossmann, Walter 53
Most, Johannes 53
de la Motte-Fouqué, Friedrich 35
Mozart, Wolfgang Amadeus 51, 52
Mühsam, Erich 53
Müller, Adam 21, 36
Müller, Heiner 83, 87
Müller, Wilhelm 42, 53
Müntzer, Thomas 6
Musil, Robert 72

Nadolny, Sten 99
Neander, Joachim 53
Neefe, Christian Gottlob 51

Complete Author Listing in The German Library

Nestroy, Johann N. 31
Neutsch, Erik 87
Nicolai, Friedrich 11
Nicolai, Otto 51
Nietzsche, Friedrich 39, 43, 48, 49, 54, 83
Novalis (Friedrich von Hardenberg) 21, 30, 39, 42

Offe, Claus 61
Oken, Lorenz 36
Olearius, Adam 7
Opitz, Martin 7, 9
Overbeck, Christian Adolf 42, 53

Panofsky, Erwin 79
Pestalozzi, Johann Heinrich 36
von der Pfalz, Liselotte 7
Pfau, Ludwig 53
Pfitzner, Hans 51
Piscator, Erwin 83
Planck, Max 82
Platen, August Graf von 39, 42
Plenzdorf, Ulrich 87
Plessner, Hellmuth 82
Preradovic, Paula von 53
Pyrker, Johann L. von Felsö-Eör 42

Quantz, Johann Joachim 51

Raabe, Wilhelm 38, 45
Radbruch, Gustav 82
Radin, Leonid P. 53
Ramler, Karl Wilhelm 9, 43
Rahner, K. 54
Ranke, Heinrich 53
Ranke, Leopold von 36, 49
Rebhun, Paul 8
Redwitz, Oskar Freiherr von 42
Reinick, Robert 42
Reinig, Christa 99
Reinmar der Alte 9

Rellstab, Ludwig 42
Reuenthal, Neidhart von 9, 53
Reuter, Christian 7
Richter, Johann Paul Friedrich 21, 34
Riedel, Carl 53
Riegel, Alois 79
Rilke, Rainer Maria 70
Rinckart, Martin 9, 53
Rist, Johann 9
Ritter, Carl 36
Rosenzweig, F. 54
Rubianus, Crotus 6
Rückert, Friedrich 42
Rülicke, Käthe 87
Rumohr, Carl Friedrich von 79

Saar, Ferdinand von 39
Sachs, Hans, 8, 9
Salis-Seewis, Johann Gaudenz von 39, 53
Santa Clara, Abraham a 7
Sauter, Samuel Friedrich 42
Savigny, Friedrich Carl von 36
Schack, Adolf Friedrich, Graf von 42
Schanz, Ludwig 53
Scheidt, Samuel 51
Scheler, M. 54
Schenkendorf, Max von 53
Schenker, Heinrich 43
Scherer, Georg 42
Schering, Arnold 43
Schelling, Friedrich Wilhelm L. 23
Schiller, Friedrich 11, 14, 15, 16, 17, 39, 42, 49, 83
Schirmer, David 9
Schlegel, August Wilhelm 21, 82
Schlegel, Friedrich 21, 79
Schlegel, Johann Elias 8
Schleiermacher, Friedrich 21, 54
Schlippenbach, Albert 53
Schlosser, Julius 79

Complete Author Listing in The German Library

Schmid, Christoph von 53
Schmidt, Georg Philipp, a.k.a.
Schmidt von Lübeck 42
Schmidt, Hans 42
Schnitzler, Arthur 38, 55
Schnurre, Wolfdietrich 99
Schober, Franz von 42
Schönberg, Arnold 51, 52
Schopenhauer, Arthur 27, 43, 54
Schrödinger, Erwin 82
Schubart, Christian Daniel 42, 43
Schubert, Franz 51
Schütz, Alfred 61
Schütz, Heinrich 51
Schütz, Helga 87
Schulze, Ernst Konrad Friedrich 42
Schumann, Felix 42
Schumann, Robert 51
Schwarz, Sibylla 9
Schweitzer, Albert 54
Seghers, Anna 87
Seidl, Johann Gabriel 42
Seuse, Heinrich 5
Sevelingen, Meinloh von 9
Siemens, Werner von 36
Silesius, Angelus (J. Scheffler) 5, 9
Simmel, Georg 61, 82
Spee von Langenfeld, Friedrich 9
Speier, Hans 61
Spener, Philipp Jacob 7
Spengler, Oswald 49
Spohr, Louis 51
Stachowa, Angela 87
Stamitz, Karl 51
Steinmar 9
Sternheim, Carl 66, 83
Stieler, Kaspar 7, 9
Stifter, Adalbert 37
Stolberg, Friedrich L., Graf zu 42
Storm, Theodor 30, 38, 39, 42
Stramm, August 66
Strassburg, Gottfried von 3
Strauss, Richard 51, 52

Strittmatter, Erwin 87
Stuckenschmidt, H. H. 43
Süverkrüp, Dieter 53
Suhrkamp, Peter 53
Sulzer, Johann Georg 43

Tauler, Johannes 5
Telemann, Georg Philipp 51
Tepl, Johann von 6
Tieck, Ludwig 30, 39, 42
Toller, Ernst 66, 83
Treitschke, Heinrich von 49
Troeltsch, E. 54
Tucholsky, Kurt 50

Uexküll, Jakob von 82
Uhland, Johann Ludwig 39, 42
Ulrich, Anton (Herzog
  Braunschweig-Wolfenbüttel) 9

Vallentin, Maxim 53
Veldeke, Heinrich von 9
Virchov, Rudolf 36
von der Vogelweide, Walther 9
Voßler, Karl 82

Wackenroder, Wilhelm Heinrich
  30, 43, 79
Wagner, Heinrich Leopold 14
Wagner, Richard 51, 52, 83
Walser, Martin 83
Walter, Bruno 43
Waltgher, Joachim 87
Walther, Johann 51
Wander, Maxie, 87
Warburg, Aby 79
Weber, Alfred 61
Weber, Carl Maria von 51
Weber, Max 43, 60, 61, 82
Webern, Anton 51
Wecker, Konstantin 53
Weckherlin, Georg Rudolph 9
Wedekind, Frank 58

Complete Author Listing in The German Library

Wegener, Bettina 53
Weill, Kurt 51
Weinert, Erich 53
Weise, Christian 7, 9
Weiss, Peter 83, 92
Weizsäcker, Carl Friedrich von 82
Wesendonck, Mathilde 42
Weyl, Hermann 82
Wickhoff, Franz 79
Widmer, Leonard 53
Wieland, Christoph Martin 10, 11
Winckelmann, Johann Joachim 79
Winkler-Oswatisch, Ruthild 82
Wittgenstein, Ludwig 54
Wohmann, Gabriele 99
Wolf, Christa 94
Wolf, Friedrich 87
Wolf, Hugo 42, 51
Wolfram von Eschenbach 2
Wölfflin, Heinrich 79
Wolkenstein, Oswald von 9
Wolter, Christine 87
Würzburg, Konrad von 4
Zesen, Philipp von 7, 9
Zetkin, Clara 41
Zuccalmaglio, A. W. Florentin von 42, 53

Titles Available in The German Library

All titles available at your bookstore or from Continuum International 15 East 26 Street, New York, NY 10010
www.continuumbooks.com

Beginnings to 1750

Volume 1
GERMAN EPIC POETRY: THE NIEBELUNGENLIED, THE OLDER LAY OF HILDEBRAND, AND OTHER WORKS

Volume 2
Wolfram von Eschenbach
PARZIVAL

Volume 3
Gottfried von Strassburg
TRISTAN AND ISOLDE

Volume 4
Hartmann von Aue, Konrad von Würzburg, Gartenaere, and Others
GERMAN MEDIEVAL TALES

Volume 5
Hildegard of Bingen, Meister Eckhart, Jakob Böhme, Heinrich Seuse, Johannes Tauler, and Angelus Silesius
GERMAN MYSTICAL WRITINGS

Volume 6
Erasmus, Luther, Müntzer, Johann von Tepl, Sebastian Brant, Conrad Celtis, Sebastian Lotzer, Rubianus, von Hutten
GERMAN HUMANISM AND REFORMATION

Volume 7
Grimmelshausen, Leibniz, Opitz, Weise, and Others
SEVENTEENTH CENTURY GERMAN PROSE

Volume 8
Sachs, Gryphius, Schlegel, and Others
GERMAN THEATER BEFORE 1750

Titles Available in The German Library

Volume 9
Hartmann von Aue, Wolfram von Eschenbach, Luther, Gryphius, and Others
GERMAN POETRY FROM THE BEGINNINGS TO 1750

Eighteenth Century

Volume 10
Heinse, La Roche, Wieland, and Others
EIGHTEENTH CENTURY GERMAN PROSE

Volume 11
Herder, Lenz, Lessing, and Others
EIGHTEENTH CENTURY GERMAN CRITICISM

Volume 12
Gotthold Ephraim Lessing
NATHAN THE WISE, MINNA VON BARNHELM, AND OTHER PLAYS AND WRITINGS

Volume 13
Immanuel Kant
PHILOSOPHICAL WRITINGS

Volume 14
Lenz, Heinrich Wagner, Klinger, and Schiller
STURM UND DRANG

Volume 15
Friedrich Schiller
PLAYS: INTRIGUE AND LOVE, AND DON CARLOS

Volume 16
Friedrich Schiller
WALLENSTEIN AND MARY STUART

Volume 17
Friedrich Schiller
ESSAYS: LETTERS ON THE AESTHETIC EDUCATION OF MAN, ON NAIVE AND SENTIMENTAL POETRY, AND OTHERS

Volume 18
Johann Wolfgang von Goethe
FAUST PARTS ONE AND TWO

Volume 19
Johann Wolfgang von Goethe
THE SUFFERINGS OF YOUNG WERTHER AND ELECTIVE AFFINITIES

Volume 20
Johann Wolfgang von Goethe
PLAYS: EGMONT, IPHIGENIA IN TAURIS, TORQUATO TASSO

Nineteenth Century

Volume 21
Novalis, Schlegel, Schleiermacher, and Others
GERMAN ROMANTIC CRITICISM

Volume 22
Friedrich Hölderlin
HYPERION AND SELECTED POEMS

Volume 23
Fichte, Jacobi, and Schelling
PHILOSOPHY OF GERMAN IDEALISM

Volume 24
Georg Wilhelm Friedrich Hegel
ENCYCLOPEDIA OF THE PHILOSOPHICAL SCIENCES IN OUTLINE AND CRITICAL WRITINGS

Titles Available in The German Library

Volume 25
Heinrich von Kleist
PLAYS: THE BROKEN PITCHER, AMPHITRYON, AND OTHERS

Volume 26
E. T. A. Hoffmann
TALES

Volume 27
Arthur Schopenhauer
PHILOSOPHICAL WRITINGS

Volume 28
Georg Büchner
COMPLETE WORKS AND LETTERS

Volume 29
J. and W. Grimm, and Others
GERMAN FAIRY TALES

Volume 30
Goethe, Brentano, Kafka, and Others
GERMAN LITERARY FAIRY TALES

Volume 31
Grillparzer, Hebbel, Nestroy
NINETEENTH CENTURY GERMAN PLAYS

Volume 32
Heinrich Heine
POETRY AND PROSE

Volume 33
Heinrich Heine
THE ROMANTIC SCHOOL AND OTHER ESSAYS

Volume 34
Heinrich von Kleist and Jean Paul
ROMANTIC NOVELLAS

Volume 35
Eichendorff, Brentano, Chamisso, and Others
GERMAN ROMANTIC STORIES

Volume 36
Ehrlich, Gauss, Siemens, and Others
GERMAN ESSAYS ON SCIENCE IN THE NINETEENTH CENTURY

Volume 37
Stifter, Droste-Hülshoff, Gotthelf, Grillparzer, and Mörike
GERMAN NOVELLAS OF REALISM
VOLUME I

Volume 38
Ebner-Eschenbach, Heyse, Raabe, Storm, Meyer, and Hauptmann
GERMAN NOVELLAS OF REALISM
VOLUME 2

Volume 39
Goethe, Hölderlin, Nietzsche, and Others
GERMAN POETRY FROM 1750 TO 1900

Volume 40
Feuerbach, Marx, Engels
GERMAN SOCIALIST PHILOSOPHY

Volume 41
Marx, Engels, Bebel, and Others
GERMAN ESSAYS ON SOCIALISM IN THE NINETEENTH CENTURY

Volume 42
Beethoven, Brahms, Mahler, Schubert, and Others
GERMAN *LIEDER*

Titles Available in The German Library

Volume 43
Adorno, Bloch, Mann, and Others
GERMAN ESSAYS ON MUSIC

Volume 44
Gottfried Keller
STORIES: A VILLAGE ROMEO AND JULIET, THE BANNER OF THE UPRIGHT SEVEN, AND OTHERS

Volume 45
Wilhelm Raabe
NOVELS: HORACKER AND TUBBY SCHAUMANN

Volume 46
Theodor Fontane
SHORT NOVELS AND OTHER WRITINGS

Volume 47
Theodor Fontane
DELUSIONS, CONFUSIONS AND THE POGGENPUHL FAMILY

Volume 48
Friedrich Nietzsche
PHILOSOPHICAL WRITINGS

Volume 49
Hegel, Ranke, Spengler, and Others
GERMAN ESSAYS ON HISTORY

Volume 50
Wilhelm Busch and Others
GERMAN SATIRICAL WRITINGS

Volume 51
Bach, Mozart, R. Wagner, Brahms, Mahler, Richard Strauss, Weill, and Others
WRITINGS OF GERMAN COMPOSERS

Volume 52
Mozart, Beethoven, R. Wagner, Richard Strauss, and Schoenberg
GERMAN OPERA LIBRETTI

Volume 53
Luther, Heine, Brecht, and Others
GERMAN SONGS

Volume 54
Barth, Buber, Rahner, Schleiermacher, and Others
GERMAN ESSAYS ON RELIGION

Twentieth Century

Volume 55
Arthur Schnitzler
PLAYS AND OTHER STORIES

Volume 57
Gerhart Hauptmann
PLAYS: BEFORE DAYBREAK, THE WEAVERS, THE BEAVER COAT

Volume 58
Frank Wedekind, Ödön von Horváth, and Marieluise Fleisser
EARLY TWENTIETH CENTURY GERMAN PLAYS

Volume 59
Sigmund Freud
PSYCHOLOGICAL WRITINGS AND LETTERS

Volume 60
Max Weber
SOCIOLOGICAL WRITINGS

Volume 61
T. W. Adorno, M. Horkheimer, G. Simmel, M. Weber, and Others
GERMAN SOCIOLOGY

Titles Available in The German Library

Volume 63
Thomas Mann
TONIO KRÖGER, DEATH IN VENICE, AND OTHER STORIES

Volume 64
Heinrich Mann
THE LOYAL SUBJECT

Volume 65
Franz Kafka
KAFKA'S THE METAMORPHOSIS AND OTHER WRITINGS

Volume 66
Benn, Toller, Sternheim, Kaiser, and Others
GERMAN EXPRESSIONIST PLAYS

Volume 67
A. Döblin, L. Feuchtwanger, A. Seghers, A. Zweig
EARLY 20TH CENTURY GERMAN FICTION

Volume 69
GERMAN 20TH CENTURY POETRY

Volume 70
Rainer Maria Rilke
PROSE AND POETRY

Volume 71
Hermann Hesse
SIDDHARTHA, DEMIAN, AND OTHER WRITINGS

Volume 72
Robert Musil
SELECTED WRITINGS: YOUNG TÖRLESS, TONKA, AND OTHERS

Volume 75
Bertolt Brecht
POETRY AND PROSE

Volume 76
Martin Heidegger
PHILOSOPHICAL AND POLITICAL WRITINGS

Volume 77
H. Arendt, K. Jaspers, and Others
GERMAN TWENTIETH CENTURY PHILOSOPHICAL WRITINGS

Volume 78
T. W. Adorno, W. Benjamin, M. Horkheimer, and Others
GERMAN TWENTIETH CENTURY PHILOSOPHY: THE FRANKFURT SCHOOL

Volume 79
Winckelmann, Burckhardt, Panofsky, and Others
GERMAN ESSAYS ON ART HISTORY

Volume 82
Einstein, Heisenberg, Planck and Others
GERMAN ESSAYS ON SCIENCE IN THE TWENTIETH CENTURY

Volume 83
Lessing, Brecht, Dürrenmatt, and Others
ESSAYS ON GERMAN THEATER

Volume 84
E. Jünger, W. Koeppen, A. Schmidt, and Others
GERMAN WRITINGS BEFORE AND AFTER 1945

Volume 86
J. Becker, G. Eich, P. Handke, and Others
GERMAN RADIO PLAYS

Titles Available in The German Library

Volume 87
Plenzdorf, Kunert, and Others
NEW SUFFERINGS OF YOUNG W.
AND OTHER STORIES FROM THE
GERMAN DEMOCRATIC REPUBLIC

Volume 88
F. C. Delius, P. Schneider,
M. Walser
THREE CONTEMPORARY GERMAN
NOVELLAS

Volume 89
Friedrich Dürrenmatt
PLAYS AND ESSAYS

Volume 90
Max Frisch
NOVELS, PLAYS, ESSAYS

Volume 91
Uwe Johnson
SPECULATIONS ABOUT JAKOB AND
OTHER WRITINGS

Volume 92
Peter Weiss
MARAT/SADE, THE INVESTIGATION,
THE SHADOW OF THE BODY OF
THE COACHMAN

Volume 93
Günter Grass
CAT AND MOUSE AND OTHER
WRITINGS

Volume 94
Ingeborg Bachmann and
Christa Wolf
SELECTED PROSE AND DRAMA

Volume 95
Hedwig Dohm, Rosa Luxemburg,
and Others
GERMAN FEMINIST WRITINGS

Volume 96
R. Hochhuth, H. Kipphardt,
H. Müller
CONTEMPORARY GERMAN PLAYS I

Volume 97
T. Bernhard, P. Handke,
F. X. Kroetz, B. Strauss
CONTEMPORARY GERMAN PLAYS II

Volume 98
Hans Magnus Enzensberger
CRITICAL ESSAYS

Volume 99
I. Aichinger, H. Bender, G. Köpf,
G. Kunert, and Others
CONTEMPORARY GERMAN
FICTION

Volume 100
P. Handke, F. Mayröcker,
Uwe Timm, and Others
CONTEMPORARY GERMAN
STORIES